POLAND, 1946

The Photographs and Letters of John Vachon

EDITED BY

ANN VACHON

WITH AN INTRODUCTION BY

BRIAN MOORE

SMITHSONIAN INSTITUTION PRESS   WASHINGTON AND LONDON

POLAND
1946

Acquisitions editor: Amy Pastan
Editor: Jack Kirshbaum
Designer: Kathleen Sims
Production manager: Ken Sabol

Library of Congress Cataloging-in-Publication Data

Vachon, John, 1914–1975.
Poland, 1946 : the photographs and letters of John Vachon / edited by Ann Vachon ; with an introduction by
Brian Moore.
p.   cm.
ISBN 1-56098-540-2 (cloth : alk. paper)
1. Documentary photography–Poland.   2. Vachon, John, 1914–1975.   3. Poland–History–1945–1980–
Pictorial works.   I. Vachon, Ann.   II. Title.
TR820.5.V33   1995
770′.92–dc20   95-17074
British Library Cataloging-in-Publication data available

Manufactured in Singapore

00 99 98 97 96 95   5 4 3 2 1

Jacket illustrations: (front) The Eyes of Poland; (back) Destroyed train station, Warsaw. Front matter
illustrations: *(p. ii)* Warsaw flea market, on the present site of the Palace of Culture, at Emile Plater Street;
(p. iii) Two Polish girls, standing beside a train. All photos by John Vachon.

The publisher wishes to acknowledge Stuart Diekmeyer, who made new prints from some of John Vachon's
original negatives for this volume.

CONTENTS

FOREWORD

JOHN VACHON, UNRRA PHOTOGRAPHER

JAN RALPH

On the ninth of November, 1943, in the East Room of the White House in Washington, D.C., seven months before the allied forces' invasion of Europe at Normandy, and eighteen months before the surrender of Germany, President Franklin D. Roosevelt, together with representatives of forty-four nations, signed the agreement to create the United Nations Relief and Rehabilitation Administration. The signatories agreed to participate according to their abilities and resources in providing relief and aid to rehabilitate the victims of German and Japanese military aggression. Two regional committees were set up—one for Europe, the other for the Far East. It was a monumental, global task in which food aid was to be the first priority.

As part of the UNRRA structure, its Public Information Division was created in April 1994 under Director Morse Salisbury, who was brought in from the same position with the U.S. Department of Agriculture. With him, one must assume there came the experience and tradition of the outstanding photojournalistic enterprise of the Great Depression years with the

Farm Security Administration. Just as the historical pictorial record of those drastic times in the American experience, initiated under the inspired hand of Roy Stryker, was designed to build support for the New Deal rescue programs, so too were the UNRRA field photographic missions launched. Where better to reach for the professionals to accomplish this task than in the ranks of Stryker's staff, which over the years had included such masters of their craft as Walker Evans, Dorothea Lange, Gordon Parks, Ben Shahn, Arthur Rothstein, and John Vachon, to mention but a few.

As the luck of the draw would have it, John Vachon was assigned to cover Poland for UNRRA, and Arthur Rothstein was sent to China. Both men have left a moving and timeless UN photographic archive of their respective assignments as an important historical record of the work of UNRRA in those ravaged countries. The UNRRA history describes "the territories administered by the Polish Government after World War II as among the most ravaged in Europe. Warsaw was a vast rubble heap." The effect of the war on the people of Poland was tragic. More than six million people died. The prewar population of 35 million dropped to 24 million by war's end as a result of the loss of the Eastern Provinces, war deaths, and exile, voluntary and otherwise. The land area of prewar Poland was reduced to four-fifths of its previous size.

John Vachon was sent to photograph the UNRRA operations in Poland in 1946. He did so with great energy and endurance, traveling throughout the country under the most difficult conditions of the postwar rehabilitation and reconstruction period. His detailed letters are an extraordinary addendum to the eloquence and skill of his camera eye. Indeed, he stands as one of the great photojournalists of his day for his entire body of work. His UNRRA coverage is a profound, unique, and special part of the United Nations story and will remain forever as a testimonial to his concern and humanity.

Jan Ralph is former chief of photography and exhibits,
United Nations Department of Public Information.

John Vachon getting a light from a soldier

INTRODUCTION

BRIAN MOORE

Warsaw in January 1946 was no longer a city. It was a grave marker at the boundary of the two very different worlds that had destroyed the armies of the Third Reich. Unlike cities in Western Europe, it had not been leveled by Allied bombardments or street-to-street battles. Instead, it had been torched and blown up, block by block, week after week, during the final retreat of Hitler's defeated army. The only part of the city which remained relatively intact was the working-class sub-urb of Praga, across the Vistula River where the Russian army had calculat-edly halted its advance, waiting coldly, in those final weeks, to ensure the death throes of the noncommunist Polish Underground's doomed last-ditch uprising against the Nazi occupation.

And so when we, members of the United Nations Relief and Rehabilitation Association, arrived on a mission to help restore the country's agriculture and industry, we entered an exhausted world filled with old and terrible hatreds and a devastation that even those of us who had already seen the results of war in North Africa, Italy, France, and Germany, could never have imagined. In this country, which in 1939 the Allies had declared war to protect, war had changed utterly the lives of its people. Now, Poland was ruled by a Polish Field-Marshal, trained in Russia, commanding an army controlled by Moscow. In addition, the towns and villages were filled with Russian troops, seen by the Poles not as liberators but as a new group of oppressors. Ostensibly, the socialist majority party ran the government, but in fact the small, distrusted Communist party was being groomed by the Russians to assume the reins of power.

I was twenty-four years old. I had landed with the British and American forces in North Africa, and then in southern Italy in the Allied invasions of those countries. I had seen collaborators shot dead in the streets of Marseilles and had traveled north to the English channel, going home amid the wreckage of abandoned German tanks, ruined farmhouses, bombed-out bunkers, and military cemeteries that littered the roads of Normandy. But now, suddenly, all of that seemed a far-away and less frightening conflict. *This* was where the decisive war had been fought in all its desperate intensity: here in Eastern Europe, which Hitler had occupied with utter contempt for those "inferior" races the Nazis tried to weaken and destroy in order to clear lebensraum for the new Reich. Twenty million Russians, soldiers and civilians, had died in the five years of struggle between Stalin's armies and Hitler's Wehrmacht. The Warsaw we were seeing was, to the Russians, simply another ruined city on the long road from Stalingrad to Berlin. This country, Poland, had been overrun in that conflict, many of its people deported to Siberia, others forced to work in German labor gangs, its cities turned into German garrisons, its boundaries redrawn, whole populations uprooted and expelled from their home territories. The scale of this war on the Eastern front mocked the aggrandising rhetoric of V-Day and our Allied triumphs. Even the Poles, who traditionally hate the Russians in equal measure as they hate the Germans, knew that Hitler had suffered his true defeat not on the beaches of Normandy but in the endless, frozen Russian wastes.

This was Poland, a country whose inhabitants looked the other way when Hitler made it his main abbatoir for the killing of six million Jews. This was Warsaw, the city whose ghetto stood like an empty concrete field, larger than the eye could measure, its only ornament the ruined brickwork of its death chimneys, a city where at night the darkness echoed to the sound of shots as military patrols, crossing the empty streets and squares, fired volleys in the air to signal to their neighbor patrols that they had reached a certain point. This was a graveyard in which, incongruously, we foreigners lived insulated from the truths of recent history. A few hotels had been used by the Germans right up to the moment of their departure. We lived in these hotels, some of us in the bombed-out splendors of the Hotel Bristol, once Warsaw's finest. We ate, often, in the once elegant Europa

Hotel, its rooms destroyed but its dining room still serving pressed duck, caviar, champagne, and chocolate soufflés. In a typically Polish contradiction, the Europa was still under the direction of its former owner, a prince whose ancestors had been Poland's kings.

But the center of our social life was, undoubtedly, the Polonia, which because of its undamaged state was crowded every night, an orchestra playing in the dining room, the bar jammed with foreign correspondents, embassy officals, and convivial drunken Russian officers offering alternate toasts to "Truman" and "Stalin." And soon in those first months among the devastated squares and toppled monuments, other restaurants came back to life, serving succulent French and Polish black market dishes. As John Vachon mentions in his letters, we UNRRA staff were provided by the Polish government with a wildly overgenerous daily allowance of zlotys, with little in the shops to spend it on. As a result we ate daily in these restaurants, like the millionaires we were not.

Shortly after I arrived in Warsaw, I was posted to Gdynia, a Polish Baltic port into which UNRRA was bringing grain, agricultural equipment locomotives, industrial machinery, and other supplies to help rebuild the economy. During the war I had served in Naples and Marseilles as an assistant to British Port officers, and back in London this was the job UNRRA had hired me to do. In my first few days in Gdynia I visited Zapot, the Baltic seaside resort John Vachon mentions in his letters. There, in the Grand Hotel, used formerly by the Germans as an R and R station, I saw an intriguing mix of black marketeers, most of them Hungarian, who gambled, wined, and wenched as though this were Monte Carlo. When I asked one of them how long he would be in Zapot, he held up a fat sheaf of banknotes and said. "I am here for 100,000 zlotys."

Within weeks I, too, left Zapot and Gdynia, recalled to Warsaw to work as a "statistical officer," a job for which I was totally unqualified. Our UNRRA mission had an overall chief, a Canadian brigadier-general named Charles Drury, and under him three deputy chiefs, one American, one British, and one Russian. The Russian, Colonel Poulnikov, was in charge of transportation and so I worked for him. To this day I don't know why I was moved out of Gdynia, and wonder what my stay would have been like had I been left there. But although I was an inefficient "statistical officer," I was delighted to be sent back to the capital.

For, above all, Warsaw was, for me, as it was for John, an exciting visual confirmation of our readings of Tolstoy, Gogol, and Dostoevsky. Here were droshka, the horse-drawn street cabs we had read about in Russian novels. Here were filthy peasants in fur-trimmed coats, driving long carts through the muddy streets: here were Russian soldiers singing gypsy chants, bearded beggars (or were they priests?) begging alms outside ruined churches. Here was the heart-stopping sound of a piano playing Chopin on a quiet Sunday morning in a deserted square. Here was a frivolous, twentyish world of elegant little tea salons rising from the ruins, at which Polish ladies in felt boots and rakish men's fedora hats, sat eating delicious pastries, drinking Polish tea in tall glasses, and chattering in fluent French as though they were in Paris in the Place St-Sulpice and not in the shadow of the huge, ugly Stalinist-architecture monstrosity that the Russians had erected on the edge of the ruined, once beautiful Warsaw Old Town.

I don't remember exactly when I first met John. In his letters to his wife, he mentions a St Patrick's day celebration. I do remember that our enthusiasm for certain books and writers forged a bond between us. We were both admirers of James Joyce and on Spring evenings we walked dark streets, discussing *Ulysses* and *A Portrait,* Auden's and Eliot's poetry, and the novels of Hemingway and Dos Passos. In his letters to Penny, his wife, which I have now read for the first time, he appears to be more unsophisticated and less politically aware than he seemed at the time. He was a handsome, rather hidden young man, uneasy with his British counterparts in the publicity department, given to quick and often naïve summations of other peoples' faults and virtues. Of course, this was his first trip to Europe and surely no country could have seemed stranger to a young American than the Poland of 1946. Like most of us at that time, his politics were left wing and he did not want to think that our allies, the Russians, were not the Soviet heroes we imagined them to be. I, on the other hand, was receiving an unpleasant education in realpolitik. Working with Polish government officials I discovered that Polish communists were almost always as antisemitic in their views as the rest of their countrymen. I also discovered that, to my communist acquaintances I was something of a joke–a socialist–a breed they distrusted more than they did the more reactionary members of our mission. I don't think John was aware of these nuances. He saw things in black and white, as is evidenced in these letters. But in the end it made no difference to our friendship, which outlasted our time in Poland and, indeed, continued for the rest of his life.

John's great and abiding gift as a photographer. as evidenced in these pictures, was his sympathy for the victims of this earth, whether they be fleeing peasants in his photographs of a village on fire, or the staring faces he encountered when he threw open the boxcar doors of a train bringing back Polish repatriates from Siberia. His photographs did not always suit UNRRA's political or propaganda purposes. They are the work of a man who had traveled all across America in the era of the Depression, recording the lives of his countrymen in those years of need, the work of a photographer who had a unique gift for empathy without sentimentality. I was told, once, that in the Library of Congress among the celebrated files of the Farm Security Administration, among the photographs of the great photographers of that era like Walker Evans and Dorothea Lange, all of them filed under headings such as farm life, industrial poverty, sharecroppers, etc., there is a special batch of photographs, a mixture of individual scenes and portraits. It is labeled simply "John Vachon Photographs" and is the only such file in the FSA annals.

These photographs of Poland, are similarly unclassifiable. They are the work of an unassuming, dedicated artist, a man whose camera eye, like the shutter box of the confessional, opened on a moment of history and recorded its truth.

Brian Moore, 1946

DEAR PENNY

LETTERS HOME, 1946

January 10, 1946.
Thurs.night
Warszawa

Dearest Penny—

It's a long time since I have written to you and I hope you'll understand the countless factors which kept me from doing so. I have so much I want to tell you, so fast things have come one on top of the other, violent changes which I've been unable to assimilate or digest. This has been a week full of real experience, and if I'd only been able to write you regularly each night I could have given you a much better picture. But anyway I would like to try and tell you the whole story.

I left England on Saturday the 5th, over Dover, cut a little corner of Belgium, and had a wonderful view of Holland—sun shining real cold glinting off these canals, and little tiny figures skating, the towns all built circularly around a tall church in the center. I didn't see any war damage until we crossed the Rhine and I knew we were in Germany. We flew about 2000 feet all the way and it was wonderfully clear. I had a terribly good look at Germany, and it was quite a sight, and I felt very strange up there in the air looking down at a country I hadn't thought I'd ever see, about a year ago. I saw lots of damaged things

Penny Leeper with John Vachon, 1937

and thousands of bomb craters in inexplicable places, but the first terrific impact was going over Hanover, and actually seeing that big city lying down there with practically no roofs over it. In a big open sort of park in the center there were several hundred people grouped together, maybe several thousand. That, they told me, was the black market. In other towns I could see similar crowds of people. We went over Potsdam, which seemed a very beautiful place, many lakes all around, and ruins of what must have been wonderful architecture.

I think Berlin must have been the most beautiful city in the world, and goddam you could weep to look at it. It was a different effect from Warsaw where you could weep to look at it, but more so you get terribly angry not at man in general, but at the Germans. But Berlin, so much bigger and grander than I'd ever thought of it, such wonderful streets, and such wonderful buildings all broken up. There is some fine modern architecture, and this heavy massive old stuff. Also the city is filled with statues and monumental groups, some terribly big and ornamental and historical looking—all these cracked in half, huge heads lying under them—all those grotesque kinds of pictures you can make of busted sculpture.

We saw the Reichstag which is the scene of the Berlin black market, and wandered around the thousands of people there—no stands or anything, just everyone milling around carrying satchels, suitcases, bundles of stuff they want to sell or trade—every imaginable kind of merchandise, cigarettes being the most sought after and valuable kind of money. Two cartons of cigarettes buys lots of types of cameras.

We went to the Reich chancellery, where Hitler lived and died, you know. It's in the Russian zone, and the guards let us right in, and we walked all through it, except we couldn't go into the bunker where he is supposed to have died. That was guarded.

Now it is Saturday night 7:00 PM. The lights went out at that last point. And this is the first chance I've had to carry on. Tonight I shall forego dinner in order to be able to write, and carry you up to the present, giving you the foundations of my observations here, my early impressions, what I've concluded at this immature date, etc. Then in the future I will try to write with fair regularity, and tell you all that goes on. But I want to advise you it's going to be hard. I live perforce much more socially here than is my wont, and expect to write less often than usual. Also mail will frequently be held up.

Now then, to carry on, I was at the door of Hitler's tomb. The Russians are still exploring in there, and don't want visitors. The Reich Chancellery is a very vast place, terribly expensive, all lavish in pink marble and minute tiles, and gold tiled eagles, it just makes you gasp at how wonderful and expensive it is, but it isn't good. I mean even if you didn't know Hitler you wouldn't care much for the guy who lived in that place.

We had a good ride all around the city. The most impressive thing to me was the people I would see, when we would stop at a corner and the passing people would look at me in the car. A man on crutches waved some marks, hollering cigarette cigarette, and two little boys about 10 were pushing a man in a sort of wheelbarrow who had no legs and his face was all twisted around in his neck. All the old women bent down double carrying these big sacks of wood on their backs. They take parts of trees in the parks, and whatever wood they find around ruins. And the damn kids acting like it's just an ordinary day of any year of any age, that really makes you cry. My God the sight of those people walking around that completely ruined city, with no look of light or anything in their eyes, the terrible idea of present misery you get when you see them, it has a sort of awful effect, you wonder who in hell you are. You are a conqueror, whether you want to be or not.

We drove through some beautiful modern housing developments, three story jobs, very like Greenbelt[1] apartments with parks, etc., and murals painted all over the sides. There too, to see them all full of holes and with no roofs, and kids playing around, it makes you sad as hell.

But to get on with my story. Tuesday we left, at 9:30 AM, and flew over Berlin, which again I saw as the most beautiful city I've ever seen, and not a roof left on it. There I could go crying again. But it's sad, isn't it, that things like that can happen to a wonderful place that people have built for so damn long. You see these terrific super highways cutting smack across the city and going way out in the country—better than the Pennsylvania turnpike, over and under passes, etc. Some bomb holes right on them.

It took 2½ hours to get to Warsaw. We crossed the Oder, and the Polish ambassador to England who had joined us that morning told me I was now in Poland, so I noted the hours down in my notebook. Across Poland the damage from the air looked nothing like so serious as over Germany. We went over some small cities and towns which had very few roofs, but not so much of the helter skelter bomb craters on the countryside. It was all flat land, all stripped out in long farms. A road with 30 poor looking hovels running straight up, farms stretching out behind. We landed 5 miles west of Warsaw, but first our pilot who hadn't been there before circled around the city, and we saw it. Warsaw is so completely wrecked, and all gone, that it's harder to imagine the city there than in Berlin. You can hardly get an idea of what it must have been like from just miles and miles of bricks and skeletons of buildings. I would think that Berlin could roughly be rebuilt as it stands but Warsaw couldn't. My first look was at a strange place I didn't know anything about, or care much about, because of my ignorance. But in my first six hours here I think I became part of the city and began to feel vaguely what the people here feel, because this is a hell of a vital place, if that's the word. It's so damn different from Berlin. The idea of its being a great city really comes across to you through seeing the people here. I was met at the airport by the UNRRA billeting officer, an English woman. It was pretty difficult to be met by her. We drove in a jeep into town and she gushed in English about the brave spirit of the people of Warsaw and of how difficult it is to get a place to live. Jesus Christ. The places I have seen people living.

Well. This is really an incredible city and I want to give you the idea of it, and don't know how I can do it. It's a big city, see. Over one million pre war. Big as Detroit. Now it is 90% *all* destroyed. A dozen or so big buildings are known as places that still stand, among them the Hotel Polonia, which was once the third best hotel in town. Now it is the best, and one of the most intact buildings. Wherever you walk here it is hunks of buildings standing up without roofs or much sides, and people living in them. Except the Ghetto, where it is just a great plain of bricks, with twisted beds and bath tubs and sofas, pictures in frames, trunks, millions of things sticking out among the bricks. I can't understand how it could have been done. They say the city was destroyed systematically, block by block and house by house. The railroad station directly outside my window was supposed to have been the finest railroad station in Europe, completed 3 months before this invasion. It was dynamited, and it's an unbelievable mass of twisted up steel, fallen walls, pieces of clothes blowing on some high girder, and messes and messes of bricks and things on the ground. It's something that's so vicious I can't believe it. Also I can't understand it.

Well anyway, I'm not at the Hotel Polonia, which is pretty damn luxurious. Eight floors; there are UNRRA offices, British Embassy offices and rooms, American Embassy, and about 1/2 of the UNRRA staff rooms. On seniority rights. I'm at the Hotel Central, a five story building. Not comfortable. No radiators. No hot water. A stinking toilet. But good looking simple furniture.

I got here Tuesday. Now it's Saturday. First I will tell you about the food because it's the first thing that hit me, so hard. And I'm too new to judge, or think, or tell you what's the score. But. You can not know, because never in my life have I seen food like you eat here. So immeasurably superior to the best restaurant I've ever been in New York or Washington there's no comparison. Breakfast: I ask for ham and eggs. Three eggs on a huge piece of ham ½ inch thick covering all of the plate. At other meals you eat thick steaks, shosh-lik, goose, wiener schnitzel, and any number of strange meat dishes, soaked in wine, the most wonderful cakes and meringues you have ever imagined. Borshcht richer and tastier than you ever dreamed. Caviar and rye bread before every meal. Vodka before dinner and after every meal. Lunch and dinner take a minimum of two to three hours each. That's the way it is, and that's the only way I've found of eating in starving Poland since I've been here. Every restaurant I go to has music with lunch and dinner, and dancing. Like the czars. And there are plenty of rich Poles enjoying themselves with the UNRRA and Embassy folk. But they've got to be awful rich. I get 1200 zlotys a day for living expenses. Meals average

Ruins of the Zamoyski Palace, with corner of the pedestal of the Copernicus statue in foreground (JV 412)

about 900 a day. UNRRA drivers (Polish) earn 75 a day. I can't grasp this whole damn thing, and I'm part of it. But either I work for UNRRA and I eat like the czars, or I don't. UNRRA here isn't an all bad organization. There are some good people in it, though it's 75% English colonials and flutter brained women. I'd been told in London "the food in Warsaw is wonderful," but I was completely unprepared for this kind of life–where all you live for, all you do is the three hour meal with music and vodka. I'm told the reason is that all around Warsaw are great farms which had a good year and have no other market for food but here, and that this is the traditional way, and always in Warsaw the rich must eat and drink in this lavish manner. But I don't understand. Anything. There's so much to try to know about. I expect to. Right now I can't help being under the spell of this wonderful food, and life here, if it's wonderful. And I brought vitamin pills with me!

Don't take my descriptions as entirely the evidence of something rich and rotten amidst starving people. It's that. But also it's the way Poland is, or always has been. It's part of the country. And the present government is part of it too. It's all so goddam much more mixed up than anything I ever thought I would run into, and where I can't explain it to you, still I'm really just getting a glimmer myself. Is it a waste of time to try to write when I have nothing to tell but my changing ideas? Tell me what you think of what I say. But you couldn't know the way it is.

Let me chronologize. I got here Tuesday. Had lunch two and 1/2 hours, with Ned Trapnell, who left Warsaw yesterday. 6:30 went to the Ballet Parnella with Dick Baradel, American. Really beautiful–a dozen ballet acts, Chopin music, jazz, folk dances, the best ballet I have ever enjoyed. Wednesday I spent eight hours eating and in the meantime went out to the airport and made photographs, with a borrowed camera of the British MP's who were arriving in Poland. Thursday I spent ten hours eating, and took some walks through the city. Friday I went on a conducted tour of the city with the British MP's, thru Old Warsaw, thru the Ghetto, and into several orphan homes, public schools, and old people's homes, making pictures of the MP's and the children and old people etc. A very good trip and look at the city. The children singing at the school made me cry again. No crap. I have cried more, like that, this past week that I have cried in the past fifteen years. These things get you. I can't tell you how it is.

Last night I developed my films in Shaw-Jones' darkroom at the Polonia, and this morning I contact printed them, and put them on the plane to England. They were OK, even though flat flash with a borrowed camera, they were better I think than most of the Polish pictures I've seen to date. Frankly. But they were no good at all–compared with the wonderful potentialities of this place. Really I have never before been in a position where it is so possible to make really great pictures.

I would like to tell you more about the set up and people here. Neither my cameras from London, nor my supplies from New York have arrived yet, in fact the cameras are lost. I can do nothing any good until I get my own stuff. It is pretty disgusting. Ned Trapnell left this morning. He is a very smart boy, and a good operator. I'm suddenly very sorry he's gone, leaving me in the midst of the British. But let me outline these people with whom I will most be associated, so that in the future when I refer to them you will know who I mean. Brigadier Drury, a Canadian, is head of the entire mission, a 35 year old energetic guy. I've hardly had a word with him yet. Polly Wallace[2] introduced me to his sister in London. She knew him in Edinburgh when he was in the army. I gather he's OK. Brigadier Brown is deputy chief, 2nd in command, a real English bastard. He wears knickers. He's really as stupid as that. He's 100% Englishman, is all I can say. He lives a happy life here. A guy named Gene Hayes, a sour faced American about 60, is chief of supplies. I've had some long talks with him. He used to be with FSA. He is, I think, the whole brains and workings of UNRRA in Poland. He is a good guy, serving difficultly under various British authorities. Insofar as UNRRA gets over in Poland, I think this guy is responsible, and I think UNRRA gets over pretty well.

Dr. Holly—medical

Miss Mott, Hayes secretary—North Carolina

Haswell, English—finance

Wilson, English—personnel

MacClanachan, the guy I met in London, the Scotsman. I work for him. We like each other very well so far. He is strictly a gentleman, and wears his uniform from the last war and has a good time. He's all right, as a guy. Politically no good.

Miss Fitch, his English secretary.

Lucy, a Polish girl who is interpreter for the Public Relation Director and who is strictly the sweet kid from my point of view. I really love her.

Miss Ashe, the wide mouthed English billeting officer.

Dick Blondell, American, medical supplies.

Irene, a Polish liaison woman, who gets you into your hotel, or gets your laundry done—by the way 6 weeks laundry for 740 zlotys, the best finished and cleanest and whitest I've ever had.

And now I come to the Shaw-Jones who are really the crux of the whole business. John and Patricia Shaw Jones. I'd been told in London a dozen times, and frequently in Warsaw, what fine people they were. They are strictly the social leaders of this set, but they are apart from the others. They are certainly the only British here who are not prejudiced. They are in fact Liberals, and akin to a type of educated New York liberals who spoke with a cultured accent I've known, that is Patty is. John is about 40, very good looking, wears a beard, is dynamic and personable, full of ideas, and not a bad guy, though I don't like him 100%. Patty is about 30. She has associated with the London theatre, is a fairly sincere good looking blonde English babe, with no prima donna about her, and I think a much better writer than John is a photographer. Anyway I can see her as being a pretty decent writer. She's OK, and thinks and talks the way English people usually don't.

I guess I will end this up now, and continue later. Thursday night Ned Trapnell asked me if I would go help him buy a camera. So I went to a shop with him. And we saw a Rolleiflex exactly like mine. I looked it over very carefully and saw it was actually in much better shape than mine, and coveted it. But I had come to help Ned pick out a camera. The price was 11,000 zlotys or $20.00, whereupon I let out a gasp. And I watched my friend Trapnell buy a better Rolleiflex than mine for two $10 bills. Today I went scrounging for one, and found a banged up one for $35–worth of course $300 in New York, but I passed it by in hopes of getting a new automatic next week for $40 from a Polish photographer I met. I can't relate to prices here. They do have everything–clothes, perfume, silverware, jewelry, cameras, food, much more so than that *Life* story indicated. And it's plenty amidst want. But I don't think people in Warsaw are going hungry, that is in a terrible starving way. They are only getting less than the minimum, like in Georgia.

I have tried to talk to several people here about the government, what will happen, the Jews, the Russians, etc. and I find those subjects absolutely closed. As UNRRA employees, members of an international organization, it is practically laid down for us that we should not talk about such things. Except Ned Trapnell who is a very intelligent guy I think, and some discussions I've had with Lucy, and a Polish photographer. My early impression anyway is that the British both abroad and in Poland spread evil lying propaganda, and that most of the things they say happen here are absolutely not true. Shootings every night they say. I will explain it to you when I get home. The English are a bunch of dirty goddam selfish liars and protectors of narrow interests, and Poland has a very good government, they are a fine people, and since I've been here I haven't seen over half a dozen Russian soldiers in the city, and this idea of Russia occupying Poland is the worst kind of lying– but that's all I heard in London.

But the thing I most want to tell you about is the life in this city–everybody. How different from Berlin, which is not half so ruined. There all people are dead, and walk with their heads down, and there are not many people about. Here all day long thousands of people on the streets, heads up, smiles, happy looks, like people who are really doing something. All around in the basements of broken buildings shops are opening up. Even in the four days I've been here there is a noticeable change. Every day this town gets more and more alive; they are cleaning away the bricks and rubble and starting businesses and walking around like real live happy people which is hard to grasp when you look at the city all shot to hell. The streets are all open, most of the sidewalks are blocked up with 8 or 10 feet of fallen stuff. This is shoveled away like snow to make an entrance to some shop a guy is opening up. And all the time they are working at tearing down and building, salvaging, etc., with no tools or machinery at all. Brick by brick they pick up whole buildings and put them into wheel barrows. How goddam little people know about things—thinking everything was so miserable in Poland. There is the misery of the food not being enough and not being distributed to enough of the people, but there is no misery of the spirit whatsoever, and if that sounds like the Polish National Anthem, it is still true—you cannot miss the feeling of the people here, who are of course going to build a greater Warsaw than ever before. It's mostly in the way they walk on the streets, fast, like they are going somewhere. We have here twelve new trolley cars, a gift from the city of Moscow, but aside from them, which really bulge, people hanging onto every part of them, there are numerous horses and wagons carrying triple loads of people for five zlotys a ride, and hay wagons full of people on top, and droshkis?, and a kind of taxi like in Central Park. I go to bed. More tomorrow.

Sunday morning–

I've read what I've written up to now, and feel I've still not adequately oriented you on just how it is here, with UNRRA. UNRRA is doing a great job, I think, by getting the stuff here. The distribution is in the hands of the government, and I can't see what need there is for the big staff that's here. About 40 people, with probably that many more due to arrive in the next month. There is a sort of small mean spirit about the staff, although they are lovely people having a gay time, they worry about who gets what, PX rations (which we get), who will get a room at the Polonia, etc. And I can't see that most of them have any work to do. Most of them seem to have no consciousness whatsoever of what UNRRA means, or of Poland, or the great things that are happening here. They live on platitudes and British propaganda. I shared my room the first two nights with a British officer, a real first water Tory. He went on to Gdynia where he will be in charge of the port. Now my room mate, permanent I guess, unless they get me a room with a bath for my darkroom, is Sig something, a Norwegian who has just come to be in charge of all communications. He is a hell of a nice guy, about my age, full of lively spirit—you know, fun. He just got out of the army, and had quite a lot of war experience, which he talks about in the right way. Ned Trapnell left orders that I was a priority case to get a room with a bath—but after his departure I haven't too much hope of this happening. He also said he was leaving his

Mishandled crates of UNRRA supplies (UNRRA 5801)

UNRRA typewriter for me, but it has got into the hands of someone else, and I'm damned if I will do any pushing or wrangling about any of this crap. I'm pretty completely disgusted with how badly they've handled me as a photographer—that stupid two months delay,[3] and getting here to find no equipment in sight. I cannot work with this borrowed graphic, which has no range finder, and is not the type I like. I cannot use Shaw-Jones' bathroom, because it's his bathroom, and it just doesn't go for me to spend long periods of time that way. It's distinctly uncomfortable. Otherwise there is no question but what I will be able to make the best pictures that ever came out of Poland. When they get me set straight I will deliver.

I got two letters from you on Thursday the 10th, mailed December 31st and January 3rd. Everyone said that was quite remarkable, and won't likely happen again. I also got a letter from my mother.

I request an occasional $10 bill if you can spare it. I will not need to draw out my $25 monthly allowance any more.

Polish is a hell of a hard language, and I'm not learning too fast, but I think I will begin to pick it up.

There is no snow at present, and it's supposed to be an exceptionally mild winter. Light is not generally very good for pictures. No sign yet of my working partner.

The dancing at the Polonia is great stuff to watch. Very fast music, and much feet stamping and whirling around.

There are a couple of twenty story buildings here which give you a slight idea of what New York might have looked like if bombed.

Please write me often and tell me what goes on.

Love.
John

————

Monday morning—January 14

Dear Penny—

It looks like it will be much easier to write you letters than to mail them. It's quite complicated. I've got to get American stamps somewhere, then put it in the UNRRA bag. I will track it down this afternoon. Tonight I am going with the Shaw Jones to a "revue." Don't know what it will be like.

I had a letter from you this morning, mailed the fifth. I'm so damn sorry that you've gone to all that trouble of preparing me a package of shirts suits and things I won't need or have room for. I was just badly informed. I will give the clothes away.

There is a fine fall of snow on the ground this morning. Last night I went out with Sig to a sort of low joint, where there were many Polish and some Russian soldiers. We had a good time, danced and drank beer. Another example of what lying nonsense the stories you hear are. I didn't tell you all the stuff I got in London: drunken Russians shooting up cafes and bars constantly. No one can go out on the street after dark. It is not safe for an American or Englishman to be seen talking with *any* Pole. This guy Sig is wonderful. He has very winning ways. And he is smart as hell. Not educated formally, but very well read. He gave me the best clearest outline of Jewish persecutions from way back before Christ down to today—all the facts, dates, reasons, results—things like that. A good sense of history he's got.

Friday I'm going to Poznan, with a borrowed camera, to photograph the lack of railroad equipment.

Love again.
J. F.

PS. Everybody here all the time bowing low and kissing ladies hands. All the time.

———

10 PM, Monday–

Dear wife–

Don't see how I'll ever get this letter mailed to you. In typical UNRRA fashion I've been given 6 conflicting stories about how to do it, and the girl who is supposed to be in charge of such things hasn't a notion. But this I know, I will require 6 cents American air mail stamps, and they are very hard to get here, so in your next letter please include about 30 of them, along with that $10 bill. And write me in London as before—pay no heed to the return address I may put on the envelope.

I had a very good walk this afternoon. God, this is a wonderful place, and I like so much to see something good like is going on all over here. It's hard, almost impossible, to get away from the British-UNRRA however. Realize—75% of the Mission is British, all of the rankest Tory type except the Shaw Jones, who are on the other hand still too damn British for me. I must sound awfully blindly prejudiced to you—you just can't understand how

Poznenska Street, Warsaw (JV 217)

much I dislike these kind of people—all of them my bosses, etc., the big shots—I have to eat with them, be nice to their women, talk and maintain friendly relations—and I grit my teeth all while I'm with them. Believe me I'm not exaggerating. A Russian officer comes into the dining room—they all stop eating and stare—"well that one's clean anyway" they say. Except the Shaw Jones who profess to like the Russians—but honest to god they're so English they do it in a patronizing way—they're always having met the most delightful Russian or finding the Poles so "picturesque." Christ you know what I mean? They're like some of the people we know in New York and Washington.

This musical revue I saw tonight was called "CIOCIA UNRRA" which means Auntie UNRRA. It really was delightful, and I use the word advisedly. It was singing, dancing, skits—which I couldn't get much out of—and the last scene was a song all about UNRRA. I didn't know the words of course, but it was very light happy stuff with six girls and a couple of men singing this fine spirited tune which expressed their appreciation of UNRRA, and was full of funny stuff and satire—not much of it was translated for me, but like: the girl got cocoa from UNRRA—she would rather they had sent her a boy. The whole revue was called Auntie UNRRA like we might call a musical "Winged Victory" or "Fourth Term Frolics" or "United Nations Fiesta"—get it?

At 7:30 I went to dinner and got back here at 10. That's really a serious problem—how damn long it takes to eat here. Everything is cooked specially for you. Your steak is brought to the table in the frying pan. I really think each item is cooked only when you order it. Tonight I had szczoslyk. You know, SHOSHLIK? Like Shish Kebab. Very wonderful.

You probably haven't heard from me for a very long time. Please let me know when you get this—and if you get it all together.[4] I go to bed. Hoping to shake off my cold. Will try again tomorrow to get it mailed.

Love—
John .

——

Thursday, Jan 17

Dear wife of the first part—

Today is Jan 17, celebration of the 1st anniversary of the liberation of Warsaw.

I am still in the same unhappy state regarding all my equipment and all my supplies. 100% disappeared and lost, and no one interested at all as to whether they will ever get here. A cable was sent to Keyser the first day I arrived, but he probably doesn't have it yet.

Cables are delayed from five days to two weeks regularly. Yesterday I wrote him a long bitching letter about the whole situation. I was not smart not to have insisted in London on taking my stuff with me. The work I can do with my Rollei and no flash, and with a Speed Graphic, half time, and not the type I like or am accustomed to, is about 6% efficient. The past few days I've been making a few shots around Warsaw, but haven't developed any yet, as I still haven't a dark room. Tomorrow I am going on a 4 day trip to Poznan, about 200 miles west of here. The main idea is to make pictures there showing the lack of railroad and railroad repair equipment. The repair equipment is coming up from UNRRA. But to me it will be an opportunity to see what I can do in this country off on the highways and by ways, my best medium. I'm going by car, with two other guys, an American and a Pole, railroad experts.

I sure don't know if you'll ever get those two letters I sent last Tuesday. It's too bad if you don't, they were such long letters. I walked around with them in my pocket for three days. Everyone told me a different way to do it, and no one knew really. I finally took them to the American Embassy, and did what the Polish girl there told me to do, and I'm really afraid there's a chance you'll never get them. Be sure to let me know. Also do not fail to send me some stamps. Six cents airmail. And a ten dollar bill.

This typewriter is borrowed from the guy next door. I wish I had one. My room mate is still Sigbjorn Skriblad, the Norwegian of whom I told you. And I think he will move with me to the room on the first floor of this hotel, at which I have a chance, which has a bathroom with no window. Also no bath tub. A very inadequate place but probably the best I will be able to find. I had a chance, which I rejected, to move into a room in an apartment of a countess, who sounds like a wrong character to be associated with. Sig is a great guy, and sings me Norwegian songs. It sure is a fine break to have got mixed up with a guy like him for roommate rather than one of those English gentlemen I might so easily have been thrown with. But I'd still much rather live alone.

Not much sense in my writing you when I'm feeling as mixed up and frustrated as I am now. This administration on UNRRA has got me pretty far down, and there is so little damn hope, unless I can some way get bold and resourceful as hell. Then the terrible waste of this beautiful picture potential, day by day, makes me sad. I sure miss a guy like Roy.[5]

Trapnell said nothing when he was here about my coming home in the Spring. I don't think it's likely. It would be sort of nonsensical to do so, as presumably by that time I will be rolling along good, or I will have quit. If I could get really started by February first, I would be ready to come home about June first, which time I propose to leave UNRRA, and build myself a good dark room in a good apartment in New York, and make a hell of a lot of money and buy a house in the country.

I told you about the Rolleiflex Trapnell bought, with my help. Dick Baradel also bought one a few days later, with my help. Same price, $20, but in much better shape, and a newer model than Trapnell's. Since then I've been looking all over for one. I have found a few old wrecks for 30 and 40 dollars. So I hold off. Today I saw a Primoflex, of which I'd never heard, but to me it looked like the dream camera, something like the Rollei, but much more beautiful. $70. I'd pretty much like to buy it, but I haven't $70.

———

Tuesday Jan 22

Dear Penny—

This is a borrowed typewriter from another guy. It's a new Remington portable, which he bought here for $25. I got home last night. Had a good trip. Left Friday morning, good sunny day, drove all day, stopped twice and took pictures in towns. It was market day. Some very picturesque places and costumes. Out in the country they wear wonderful multi-colored clothes. We stayed 3 nights in Poznan, 300,000 pop. Wonderful old city hall undamaged, 15th century. Photographed in a railroad repair shop, a locomotive factory, very huge place, and a rubber processing and manufacturing plant. All places which hope to get UNRRA machines or raw materials. Think I got some good pix. Don't know how this dopey outfit will ever use them though. Traveled with Douglas Cannon. My god he is a naive super-American. Terribly bountiful and patronizing. However he's the best guy I can figure out to travel with at present, and I hope to spend most of February with him visiting coal mines, steel mills, oil fields, refineries. He is the industrial rehab man, and that kind of work hasn't really started yet at all. He is going on an inspection trip. After that I will work 100% on agriculture and rural life, when spring comes. Also on this trip was Karl Juraz, a Pole about 50, member of the ministry of transport, on loan to UNRRA. Hell of a nice guy. His family lives in Poznan and we visited them at some length. A wife and daughter. Also lots of photographs of the old days, their house in Warsaw—he was apparently pretty well off—and their other daughter, Krystyna, who was shot by Germans when she was 17. Now they live in 2 rooms in Poznan. Some photograph albums and some books were all they saved from Warsaw. I met lots of people in Poznan I don't have time to tell you about now, but will when I see you. The matter of fact stories you hear over and over about people being killed are awfully staggering, but become so they almost roll off you. There just isn't anyone who doesn't have his own story of tragedy to tell you.

I don't know what this is all about, because she couldn't speak English. But I agreed to do it. I think it's a girl who wants to come to America. So. Will you please find Stefan Karmiuski or Karminsky, or the closest you can get to that, at Hokar or Holzar or Hattar Products Corporation, 82 Hall St., New York.[6] And tell him to send the papers to Zofia Nawrocka, Jacowkiego 21/11. Poznan, Poland.

I haven't been to the office yet today, but I spent all morning writing a memo to Mac, telling him what I think I should do now. I have been advised that my two cases of equipment are here now. Not the supplies, but all the camera stuff, so I am pretty happy. And anxious to get to work good. Today I've felt a little lousy with the tail end of a cold, that's why I'm staying in. I was out a lot on this trip I just finished. Word is that the dark room downstairs is off again, but now there is a prospect of a private room and bath in a private apartment in town. I'm sure anxious to hear from you now. And to learn whether you've been getting my letters. If I get a room of my own, I'll have much more opportunity to write, I hope. Still, I want to spend most of my time traveling. Please write to my mother and tell her how it is about me writing. Downstairs here they drink vodka for breakfast. Always the bottle of vodka is on the table, and you pay according to how much you take out.

Love
John

———

Wed. Before dinner

Dear Pen –

The only thing that mars my happiness here is that I have so little or no chance to write or mail letters to you, or packages. I won't get this mailed tomorrow either, because I've got to go out on a farm all day with the agricultural man. To get a postage stamp is quite a job. I'll have to go over to the Embassy, and they don't like to sell them, so please hurry with sending those. I do so much hope my first long letter to you wasn't lost, because it set the locale here, and it would be so hard now to have to do that all over. As I recall, most of my observations in that letter remain accurate, except I believe I said I hadn't seen more than half a dozen Russian soldiers. That's not true. There are lots of Russian soldiers. I didn't recognize them at first. But most of all–this is a great city, really. It gets right into ya. All the little restaurants where you go, people playing the piano. Chopin you are hearing all the time, and I'm getting to love it. It reminds me of sitting home on the sofa while you play Chopin. Only here it's more to the point. Lots of other wonderful music, mazurkas, etc. and really music everywhere. A hell of a musical city. All I told you in that first letter about British, Russians and Poles still stands as far as I can observe. Except I've got a few new slants on the real essence of this Russo-Pole antagonism. I would like to write to Roy and the Delanos,[7] but all I want to tell them is all that stuff I wrote you last time, so let them read that letter please.

My pictures of British MP's visiting Polish children were published in the *London Times,* I'm advised, and everyone is just happy as hell about it. The greatest thing that could have happened. In fact, according to standards of work accomplished here, I now have every right to sit back and do nothing for at least six weeks. The Shaw Jones remain a lovely couple, at least John is a decent sort of chap. He just isn't a photographer though. Maybe that's what makes my stuff look over-good to me. His wife, Patricia, is the person I like best on this whole mission. That is she seems to me smarter, she thinks more down my alleys than anyone else here. And confirming my growing prejudices, I find she isn't an English girl at all. She was born in County Cork.

All day today I worked in the Shaw Jones bath and dark room. Developed six dozen 4 X 5 films from Poznan. While there is nothing really terrific there, it's all good enough, some kind of good, and generally useful. It suffered some from John's lousy developer. But I'm stuck with that until my trunk arrives. Friday I will probably develop all day. The stuff I do tomorrow, and seven rolls of Rolleiflex from Poznan.

I got my raincoat back cleaned. It's a beautiful light color exactly like when it was new. These Poles sure do a fine job of washing and cleaning.

I haven't had a chance to go out buying Rolleiflexes since I've been back. Last night the Shaw Jones had eight letters for me. One from Jack Crocker of Dublin, one from Lew Gittler[8] of Paris, who says I should come work for Life, one from Ted Lebow, and five from you all, including the bunch of clippings, mailed January 5. Haven't had a chance to read them all yet.

The personnel here is growing with every plane that comes in. Four Norwegian girls. A New Zealander. There is but one Russian on the mission. A pretty big shot, whom I haven't met yet. They tell me he is a wonderful guy. The English say he is not at all like a Russian.

You really lay me low. Telling me to destroy a sheet of your letter in which you discuss what you have been reading about Poland. You too have been under the influence of Hail Britannia. Honest, not a single member of the secret police has searched my room since I've been here. But right here, among enlightened Americans, you will hear such stories. And the Hotel Polonia is fully wired with a dictaphone system.

Now I read you are sending me food. Which of course I don't need. But how could you know. The one food that would be welcome would be some more of that Barrington Hall instantly prepared coffee, which I bought at Gimbels. I've nearly used up my one can of it, and given my other can to the Shaw Jones. Have I ever told you about the meringues and cakes they have here? Warsaw is supposed to be the best city in the world for such things. They are unbelievably good, and various. All full of butter and rum and stuff. Once we get communications established here I'm going to send you a little number I've bought, he says modestly. My god. And I would like to get from you coffee, fountain pen, clippings, pictures of you and children, stamps, $10 bills, letters.

I went to a movie one night in Poznan with the Juraz family. It was "The Grey Lord," the first English or American movie to be in Poznan since the war started, and everyone was all stirred up about it. It was a very very bad movie, but I enjoyed the Polish news reel immensely. There are Russian movies to be seen in Warsaw, which I hope to see lots of.

Tell me what kind of things you would like me to buy you if I could find them. I really think I could find anything here. For instance electric irons, all sizes and varieties are plentiful.

Thursday night, 10:30–Just now back from a great day in the country with Gene Hayes, and an Ed Michowsky, agricultural man, a genuine Wisconsin farmer, and the Polish Minister of Agriculture. It wasn't much for pictures. I just went along to make some straight technical shots of stallions for Hayes to take back to Washington to prove something or other. But we had a wonderful time. The country around here is flat, much like lots of the Dakotas only much more populous, and villages more frequent. And more trees. Still it often looks just like Dakota. Today was a fine sunny day. Cold as hell. This is providentially the mildest winter anyone can remember. There is no snow except little left over patches. It is quite cold though, but bracing. All the ponds and lakes frozen–it's very beautiful out in the country. Today we visited three state breeding farms–horse breeding. All of them were lavish old estates–really palaces. One was where Napoleon stopped on his way back from Russia and had a son by Madame Viskusa. Wonderful statues and pictures in these places. We left at eight AM and got to the first farm about ten, where, after pictures and inspection we had a little tea; vodka and beautiful homemade sausages. About two, at the second farm we had lunch. Four different kinds of vodka. Their hors d'oeuvres took about an hour–head cheese, pickled mushrooms, some little fish, and a variety of meats. Then borscht. Then came the steaks. Tonight we were at Napoleon's place for dinner. A soft footed attendant taking your plate away and filling it up every two minutes. String music playing, the electric lights going way dim or failing constantly–we had the usual hour of hors d'oeuvres, then fish, then some slabs of juicy fowl. I don't know what–they just squirted out at you as the fork went in, terribly tender and good. That stuff is all the Polish Way. Very nice people we were with at all these places–the farm managers and secretaries and their wives—government people. I admired horse beauty like I'd never done before—real magnificent animals, white Arabians, and those fine snappy streamlined red ones. At each place the horses were brought out for us and paraded around the grounds, each one with an attendant—either an old man or quite a young boy—all obvious horse lovers. The old men bow low to us, and take off their caps sweepingly. We bow back and say *dzein dobry.*

Tomorrow I will develop all day, and I hope I will get this mailed.

Sig is out tonight. I have drawn some pictures and hung them over his bed. It gives the place a homey touch.

I am very happy here—in my prospects of doing some wonderful work. If only my supplies arrive soon. Anyway I'm happy here. It's a fine place to be, and the Poles are great people.

LOVE
JOHN

━━━━━

Wednesday—January 30

Dear Penny:—

It's snowing out, quite beautifully, and I should be out getting some good pictures but I'm not. I still live in the Hotel Central on the sixth floor—we walk both ways. Tomorrow I expect to move to the first floor, probably with Sig, where there is a room in which they have installed a bath tub for me. And finally I will have a dark room. But all UNRRA will no doubt want to take baths in my tub.

I been lying here thinking out long letters to you. Now it's not coming so flowingly, when I have to write. I still haven't heard from you since you heard from me, if you get what I mean. I want to know how long it takes, etc. And in case any letters were lost: Repeat request: thirty 6 cent airmail stamps, please send me.

I been lying here thinking about how happy I was on all my various photographic assignments for Roy, really feeling longing for those good old days—that February and March '42 in Dakotas and Montana though, that is always my very happiest memory. Next winter Penny, honest, for sure—I must get out there again. Maybe you can come with me. I've been thinking a lot about Roy lately. For one thing, I'm realizing how really damn much he means to me—the old father stuff. I think little or lightly of that at home, but it's really true.

21

Stallion on a state stud farm near Gostynim (UNRRA 4224)

I practically love the guy. Then also, I'm realizing that the way I'm trained I can work well only by working for him—that is real well. I can fill the requirements on this or any job, but to get good satisfaction out of it, I've got to work for Roy. So I want to again, at the earliest opportunity. I hope he will soon open up another shop.

I guess I am homesick as hell right now, thinking about all the people I like and can't be with. You and Ann and Brian. Roy. Jack and Irene, Esther, my mother, Sol and Feely.[9] Those are the people I like, and it's very stupid to undergo enforced absences from them. I feel it here because there are no real good friends here. There are some nice people, but none of them quite exactly my kind of people for real good friends. Next time I get back with you Penny we will make everything work, and not let anything go wrong. Because I love you more than I know, and you are the mainspring of my life. And also you are a very good fine girl.

I can't tell you anything that makes much sense except that I love you terribly much and I want to be with you, and I have a great hope for a lot of happy future we are going to have, and even if we don't become much different when we get back together, it is still a great happy future just for us to be together some more the same way we've always been.

My unfortunate surname Vachon. Cow in France, wecz, pronounced VASH in Polish, means "little louse." That's what I'm being called to distinguish me from *John* Shaw Jones who has the priority on John.

One of these days, after I see if you ever really get my mail, I'm going to enclose you a dozen or so negatives with a little description, to ask you to get some beautiful prints made, to get me a story in *Popular Photography* or *US Camera*. I'm quite anxious to do that. Let people know I was in Poland, in case UNRRA never lets it leak out.

Since I last wrote you I've made a few more shots around Warsaw, and some dopey UNRRA stuff in a broadcasting studio. But I'm not working right at all yet. That is I'm not on anything, not going anywhere. I'm really surprised at how good I am—I mean competent—you know. It's a cinch for me to give UNRRA here anything they want or ask for. Trouble is nobody wants anything much. But don't worry—I'm going to get to work and give them plenty that they don't know they want.

love
John

Maybe you better start using the address on this envelope. It only costs six cents.

———

Family at the dinner table *(from left to right):* John's daughter, Ann; his mother, Ann; wife, Penny; and son, Brian. Photographs in background include *Migrant Mother* by Dorothea Lange and *Painted Door on Barn* by Jack Delano.

Dear Penny:

Didn't I just write to you yesterday? And here I am, writing again. This should be the 6th envelope you have received. Let me know if you have. Today the plane came in, and I got a letter from you and Ann, and a valentine from Polly. Not from Phil and Polly.[10] Just from Polly. Also on the plane which came in was Mr. Redfern, the chief of the Public Relations Department. At one sight of this guy, the last hope is fled. He's about 60. American. Spent 15 years at the embassy here before the war. Just exudes the breath of State Department Toryism. Why in Gods name they should send a guy like that here I can't understand. I've described MacClanachan to you, I think, but I've since learned that he is really worse than I described him–that is his ideas are worse. For instance, he's anti-Semitic. So get the picture. It's important. Two doddering reactionary old fools run the department I work for. My Polish speaking partner Yashakowsky has been delayed because he was refused a visa by the government, because his father was editor of a violently anti-Lublin and anti-Soviet publication. But now he has been granted a visa, and should turn up in a few weeks. Pretty picture in all, hey? I get to like the Shaw Jones more every day–they do have good attitudes–but I can't ever go 100% all out for them. They are just a little too much "these quaint Polish people" for me. But they are good honest kind people, and certainly my only refuge here.

I'm perhaps not explaining to you exactly what's wrong with the Shaw Jones. Patty is what you might call a stunning looking girl, and John is a tall handsome guy with a beard. They both wear resplendent uniforms, and occasionally Patty puts on a white fur coat, and John a great shaggy fur coat. They are well liked by people–Poles everywhere we go greet them with great enthusiasm and warmth. But they are just too damn conspicuous. They are a little like Great People among these Poor Peasants. John is always giving money to beggars–which for some reason embarrasses me to see him do–if you can get what I'm trying to point out. With all their real kindness and liking for people, they seem to lack the warmth and real even terms with people which I think a photographer has got to have, and which is a reason why I think the Delanos would be so perfect here.

Now about me: as I said before, if I can get the ball rolling, I can do some wonderful work here. And I definitely will either get the ball rolling or quit. I won't sit around on my butt here and live with the idle rich. It's really a pretty shameful business here. The number of English gentlemen is increasing with every plane that comes in. The staff has nearly doubled since I arrived. They get in people to take care of the people they get in.

I forgot to tell you about a Russian-Polish guitar player whose acquaintance I have made in a restaurant–a really very nice guy, and I think one of the best singers I've ever heard. Really a voice, you know, like concert stage, and a personality in the songs like Jolson and Chevalier and better, and he sings little fast songs like Burl Ives or Richard Dyer Bennett, but so far superior, and also long loud songs, full of shouting. Anyway, him, his name is Sasza Nievski, and the piano player, who is also a nice guy, I have *promised* to get some music for. They really are longing for new music, not having seen any for six years. What they want is: *Rhapsody in Blue,* Debussy, Plesow–don't know that one. Sasza: words and music to *Night and Day,* and 3 or 4 other good popular American songs of the past few years. Will you please fill that request? As well as you reasonably can? And get it to me as soon as possible? I wrote to the Delanos, and asked them to send me some cowboy songs.

Tomorrow is the day I will get my contact prints from 134 negatives I left with a guy to print. This is something of a first milestone in my stay here. I will learn 1) whether I can count on decent contact prints here, and thus how good my stuff will be able to look to people here who don't know anything about pictures or how to look at contacts, and 2) I will learn what kind of impression I will make on the powers here, and whether they think I have gone needlessly astray in photographing farmers' markets and Russian monuments and children in the street and all without any possible UNRRA connection.

Tonight I'm in my new room alone, but I'm not very happy. It isn't a very clean room, like the one upstairs was. I think maybe I'll try to move back, and walk down 6 flights when I want to use my dark room. Which isn't ready yet anyway.

Love
John

———

Saturday–

Here I am again, another day, and haven't mailed my Bonny's letter. I have no stamps. I'll do it on Monday though, sure enough. Tonight I am staying in to write letters, and I've had my dinner and a bottle of vodka sent up. All day today I worked in the Shaw Jones' dark room, developing Rolleiflex rolls. And my God wife. I am a good photographer. I don't know how useful UNRRA will find this stuff, but it's good pictures. Roy would like them. Farmers standing around under the new Russian monument at Ludowic, and old women carrying pails of water past broken down tanks on the main street of Kutno, and etc. Really damn good pictures. And it's a crime if they don't get used.

This UNRRA mission staff here is crystallizing more and more for me. Frankly there aren't too many *good* people on it. I've mentioned Mac to you, I think. He's my boss. Mac-Clanachan. Well he's a nice enough guy. Pleasant. A gentleman. But in so far as he thinks, he is a TORY. But he doesn't think much, and he is impossible to reach on anything serious. He can grasp no idea of what I want to do here, or of what good things could be done here. My long careful memo to him just rolled off him like water off a duck's back. But he isn't much of an obstructionist, and if I could get rolling I don't think he'd do me any harm. But nowhere in UNRRA do I see the opportunity for real good use of what I might do, and there is certainly no chance of any intelligent direction, or even sympathy with my aims. The good people here, so far as I know up to now, are the Shaw Jones. Fine people. John is a hell of a nice guy, and smart too. Patty is really 100%, a very good gal, with good ideas. She is certainly the whole guts of the PR setup here. We three have formed practically a little clique here, anti all the British Lords who run the show here too much. We get along fine and have a good time together. Gene Hayes, the American, ex FSA, is another good man. He is not anti-government, like most of this staff is. Sig, my room mate, is a good boy — a little heavy handed on the thick Norwegian humor sometimes, but really a fine fellow. Milchowsky, the Wisconsin farmer, is OK, but sort of anti Russian, like a good Pole. But otherwise, nearly everyone, except some of the Polish employees, is a guy who shouldn't be here representing the United Nations.

Here is a picture of me when I was photographing the British MP's visiting orphan homes. The guy next to me is the British air attache here. A Polish photographer made this and gave it to me.

I got another letter from you yesterday, mailed Jan 17th. It's my 18th letter from you since I left the USA. Happy Groundhog's Day.

John

▬▬▬▬

Sunday — Feb 3

Dear Penny —

I received two letters from you today, and one from my mother. You still hadn't heard from me in Poland, and I'm afraid my fine long first letter was lost. When I learn for sure I will start over and give you a briefing on Warsaw, the UNRRA mission, etc.

I have moved back into my room with Sig on the top floor, and finally decided to call this home. We are buying an electric cooking plate, lamps, mirror, eating utensils, etc. My

John visiting an orphanage, with a British air attaché

dark room on the first floor is still not ready, but will be this week. I got my contact prints back, and they really are god awful. The negatives are good—but printed on this old paper they all come out a dirty grey, scratched, stained, just horrible. So I won't make a very good showing, I regret. I've decided I'll have to make my own prints. Probably build a contact printer. My respect for my own knowledge and abilities along photographic lines has grown tremendously of late.

I had a wonderful time last night. I went out alone—which one very seldom does here—to the Konga, where are the singer and pianist I wrote you of. The singer was not there last night, so I spent all my time with the pianist, and got to know him quite well. He's a very good fellow, and a real honest to God artist. He and I and a waitress stayed in the place until 2 AM—three hours after it closed, playing piano nearly all that time, with a few respites for drinking vodka. He played dozens of Beethoven sonatas, beautifully, and powerfully. And what a guy to look at while he's playing. He's about 25, and good looking. He gets rapt ecstatic looks all over his face while he plays. He studied at a conservatory in Poznan, if that conveys you anything. My Polish is getting on quite well, I think, especially when I go out like this and get with Poles alone.

There's so damn much to do here Penny, I feel pretty awful when I think how I've as yet done nothing, and how there's a chance I'll end up doing nothing.

I'm anxious to get pictures of you and the kids. And by all means a clipping from *US Camera*. And any reading matter you can happen to pick up. I'd give a thousand zlotys for a copy of *Time*. Always advise me of world news, as I really do miss it.

There's quite a tender and deep bond of friendship—pal stuff, you know, between me and Sig. Only he gets on my nerves terribly at times. I like to be alone, ya know. But now I see it's really better to be living with someone. This is very much like with Feely in Washington. That is lots of the same situations, feelings, problems, come back to me. It isn't very much like living with you. That's different. Sig sings and is merry in the morning straight off, which annoys me. He tickles my toes if I don't get up. He is 37 years old, but looks and seems about 27. Nice looking guy, blond*ish*. Slight bald spot growing on top, but he still seems very young. I really believe possibly Scandinavians mature late or something. Anyway he tells me he was very late growing up. He's told me an awful lot about himself. He's unmarried but is looking for a wife—seriously, that way. He has a quite different code of—? attitude, belief, good and bad, values, etc. from me. That's what makes us interesting to each other. Despite his merry nature, he is a very serious guy: bonds, honor, friendship, etc. He kind of looks like a sailor. I'm really damn glad I got to know him, and very lucky to live with him rather than someone else.

One drinks a lot here, you know. Impossible place for an alcoholic. I'm not doing too badly, and I don't think you would be at all ashamed of me. I probably have some vodka nearly every day, but don't do any heavy stuff that I have great regrets for. I've been pretty good and tight two or three times, was quite sick one night, but all in all I'm not being a bad boy. Like last night I gradually got moderately plastered. But it was all OK, didn't get sloppy at all−even though I did kiss a Russian officer on both cheeks whom I met on my way home. I guess a good point is that here you always eat a lot when you drink.

Please write to me a lot of long letters, telling me all about everything. Just go easy on descriptions of movies you saw, clothes you bought for the children, and a few things like that. Tell me about yourself, and about other people. I like to hear about what everyone does and says.

Did I tell you about when Mr. Wilson, our British Personnel officer, remarked about when he was playing in Berkeley Square several years ago, I floored him by saying "Supposing you were in a boat, going down stream. You saw some violets along the bank−" He took it from there and finished it. Really floored him though.

O God how I wish I could get to work. And the longer I don't, it soon gets to where it's my own fault, you know. I feel a lack of push and drive which I should have, to go out and do great things, forgetting the damn UNRRA personnel. Believe me it's a sorry mess here as far as people go. Except: Shaw Jones, Sig, me, Gene Hayes, Malchewsky, some Poles, Polnikoff, Simon,−everyone here is reactionary, stupid, malevolent, petty. And there are a hell of a lot of them.

Love
John

———

Mon, Feb 11 ?

Dear Penny,

Haven't written you for about a week. In fact I had no chance to mail the letter I wrote you last weekend, as I was whisked away to Danzig. So yesterday I gave it to a major who was leaving for home, and he will mail it, perhaps in New York, and you should get it fast. But it will be old.

I had two letters from you awaiting me when I returned. I'm very bothered and worried about your not having heard from me yet, as of January 30. And I anxiously await your first letter after you hear from me. And I need stamps terribly. And some $. I got your letters sent regular to the Polonia, but I think APO in London is better.

Prices have gone up. $ have gone down. But I saw a most magnificent spanking new Ikoflex this morning for $60. My Rollei is not in too good condition, and I'm most anxious to buy an automatic.

Last Monday night into whom do I run in the lobby of the Polonia but Les Atkins[11] I sure was glad to see him. He's a good guy. I appreciate him as I never did before. Get the picture? We went over to the Konga and heard the piano. Sasza, the singer, is no longer there. Then we came back to the Central—Les stays here too—and had a very large night of it in Madeline's room, with about twelve people, vodka, coffee, and a guitar which Dick Baradel bought, and much song fest.

Then Tuesday morning I left for Gdynia and Gdansk with Gene Hayes and a veterinarian from New Zealand, quite a decent bloke.

——

Tuesday night.
Same week.

Today, all day, 9 AM until 7 PM, I was in Shaw Jones dark room, and developed all of my Gdynia-Gdansk. Pretty fine stuff, I might interlope. I haven't gone out for a meal all day—ate K rations 3 times. They give them to us when we go on a trip. I eat the cheese, meat, eggs, biscuits, coffee, soup, and save the candy, gum and cigarettes to give to people I take pictures of.

But about my trip, I will tell you at least briefly. From here to Gdynia we did in nine hours, following the Vistula all the way up. The country gets rollier and hillier, and it's very nice to look at. Big wooden windmills, wayside shrines, ancient looking little villages on the river, etc., my kind of landscape—but I didn't have a chance to do anything all the way up. It wasn't my trip. We stayed in Zapot, midway between Gdynia and Gdansk. Gdansk you know is Danzig. All three are within 15 kilometers. Gdansk, like Berlin, hit me very strong as a beautiful city. It's badly damaged, but it's still very beautiful. Long spacious avenues with straight lines of big trees with their tops shot off. It's a very German place in looks, atmosphere, etc. Many Germans, I guess all, have been moved out, but people still talk German there. Some wonderful old buildings on the canal, railroad station, ancient grain elevators, etc.

Zapot was a pleasure city—home of Poland's most famous gambling casino. Gdynia was a very new modern, all modern, little city. Very good looking. None of these places look like Warsaw, because the method of, and reason for their destruction was different. But they're all shot to hell, very little left. We went on lots of boats up there in the two ports, and drank whiskey with the captains. Photographed: UNRRA grain and UNRRA cattle being unloaded. The cattle was a swell story: The United Brethren, a religious group in the U.S., of which I'd never heard, together with some Amish and Mennonites, had pledged a cow apiece from their farms to give to Poland, via UNRRA. Some 600 cows were on this boat, and with them about twenty young Brethren, Amish, and Mennonites who came over to tend the cattle on the trip across. They were all conscientious objectors, ages as young as 15 or 16, up to about 30, but most of them 21, 22 year olds. Very nice bunch of boys, acting just like Americans, whistling at the Polish girls, etc., and not seeming at all conscientious or Amish. Many of them were from Lancaster county, Pennsylvania. Others from Ohio, Indiana, one from Glencoe, Minnesota—near Bob's farm.[12] The Polish government gave them an all day trip around the countryside to see where their cows went, and I followed, photographing them on farms, at an agricultural school, playing with a destroyed German tank in front of a barn, etc. Very good set of pix, I think.

We went out one night in Zapot with the captain of the port and four non-English speaking Polish girls, very nice girls. I conversed a lot with my pocket dictionary, and turned up one very amazing bit of new knowledge. I had whistled a tune to this girl to ask her the name of it, and was told that to whistle, in Poland, is "rude" "shocking" "improper" except in the privacy of your own room. That's true, too. I've noticed people in the streets turn around to stare at me as I've walked along whistling.

Coming back we cut west from our route, and spent the night in Bydgoszy, a city of over 100,000, practically undamaged. Visited an agricultural college here, met a fine man, a food scientist with one arm, who showed us his library, books all muddied up and torn, and his notes which he had saved—half burnt, wet and smeared, foot marks on them, etc. The Germans had occupied this building while he was in a concentration camp. We went by one of those concentration camps outside a town, very bleak and ugly looking with elaborate barbed wire devices all around it.

Like I said, my negatives look damn good. It was quite an unhappy trip, though, because for all the wonderful things to photograph on the way through, I could stop for none. Only when I got to the Gene Hayes locations could I get to work. O how I wish Roy worked here.

I made a picture of a chimney sweep. A real individual profession in Poland. He wears black clothes, is black all over, carries a funny looking rope and brush, and a tall black top hat on his head. He reminds me very much of some story I read as a child, probably Hans Christian Anderson.

No letter from you in the bag today. Maybe you still haven't heard from me, and are mad, and won't write no more.

Members of the cattleboat crew, who tended the livestock sent by the Church of the Brethren and Mennonites in the United States (UNRRA 4229)

Chimney Sweep, a photograph used as a family Christmas card

I got back from my trip Saturday about 5 PM, and that night we all, everybody in UNRRA practically, went to a dance given by the Ministry of Health, and I got home at 8 AM. So did everybody else. Les had a wonderful time. He can get so well into the spirit, and dance mazurkas and stuff good. I can't dance worth a damn.

My dark room is still undergoing alterations, work bench being built, me trying to find stray pieces of equipment, and arguing with people that they cannot bathe there. It won't be ready for use for another week. And then it won't be much good. Not as big or convenient as Shaw Jones'.

I expect to spend all the rest of next week developing, printing, and arranging for my new dark room.

Next Monday I plan to go on a trip south with Leslie: Lodz, Katowice, Krakow. To see UNRRA medical supplies in use in hospitals. and to find a US Army doctor delousing repatriates with a spray gun. This should be a good trip, as with Les I'll feel freer to stop a lot en route, and maybe be able to get pictures in the old FSA manner.

I must sometime tell you about a lot more people here, and more about the social life. This is per force social life such as I've never before experienced. There's very little of it I like, but it's impossible to avoid a great deal of it. For instance, I have danced more this past month than in the previous two years. And one thing I've learned for sure and am resigned to: I can't dance no good. Except by myself. Also we sing a lot. And I learn that I can only sing good when I can be the leading part.

Les makes references to you all the time, about how wonderful a wife you are, how I've got something there, you're one in a million, etc. Now don't you regret your frequent caustic references to Les? He's really a pretty good boy, as far as someone doing a job—compared to everyone else around here. I read him that fine letter from Brian—That really was a fine one. Les expects to start for home in about two weeks—arriving about a week hence, stopping in London and Paris en route.

I see you're sending me sugar and tea. Nice. I can use them. But not necessary. Except powdered coffee. That I need. Every Friday we get PX rations. 1 carton cigarettes. 1/2 bar soap, and from time to time coffee, tea, jam, toilet paper, tooth paste, blades, etc. This stuff by the way will be charged up to me, and I will owe it all when I get home. Our per diem is being raised to 1800 zlotys per day. That's pretty disgusting.

I hope you'll send me the Pan American magazine with my pitchers. I sure wish I had those color pictures and some other pictures of you. All. As soon as I hear from you that you've heard from me: I'm going to send you a dozen or so negatives, and ask you to get some nice prints made, and get Roy's or someone's advice, and write a little bit of stuff, and get me a story in *US Camera*. So I will have prestige. I want to be sure to get something like that, at least, out of this visit. I've discussed this with Redfern, and he says quite OK, only be sure to mention UNRRA, say something nice about them. One or two of the pictures will be definitely UNRRA. You angle it all.

My goodness but your letters are full of radio programs. Nice touch of home, I suppose. Would you like me to buy you some music? Chopin, Scarlatti, Beethoven and etc etc etc are for sale on the streets, old copies of things found or looted or something. Very cheap. Tell me what you'd like. I'm just not a good buyer like other people. They all buy pictures, clocks, jewelry, amber, cameras, chess sets, statues, watches. With me it's like with flowers—I enjoy seeing the stuff around but never think of getting it for myself. I've seen in some of the small towns, wonderful paintings, like primitive Americans, of cities and farms etc. Really wonderful. But how could I buy a painting to take it home? Would you like some pretty cups with Polish eagles on them?

These last few pages have been interrupted frequently with conversation with Sig who is confiding me all about his hopes and dreams and his sex life. And a visit from Les Atkins who finished off my bottle of vodka, and told a few of his funny stories. Jeez it's funny, and sort of comfortable, to find an old fart like him here. He's going to call you up when he gets back.

I told you about one of my pictures being in the *London Times*—they all got very happy about it, because the *Times,* only four pages, uses very few pictures, and only real good ones, and this was used just with a brief caption, no story about the MP's at all. So they think I must make good pictures. Also, I've learned, several other London papers used others of that set.

A cable came from Washington last week asking for motion picture footage on Poland. Very vague, but we assume it's to be put into a movie they're making on UNRRA in general. I have very deliberately avoided all opportunities of being associated with it at all. I think that wisest, if I'm to get my job done around still lines. A Polish camera man is going to shoot it. The Shaw Jones will work with him, not shooting, but directing and researching. I have asked to be excused from it completely. But don't think I'm not going to be in this movie stuff sometime.[13]

Love
John.

———

Dear Penny–

I got two letters from you a few days ago, and now you've heard from me, for you send stamps and ten bucks, for which thanks. You might renew those stamps right away, as I owe a good many of them, and they are very difficult to obtain here. Also another ten sometime would do no harm.

Also had a letter from Polly Brown who enclosed an article from the *New Republic,* January 7, by Irving Brant, "Eyewitness in Poland." You might like to look it up. I think it's very good and fair and accurate.

I haven't yet received the suit you mentioned, and possibly won't. It seems lots of mailed packages never get here, pilferage along the line. Write via London or APO for best results.

We don't exactly have a PX as you seem to think. We get in some PX supplies. A carton of cigarettes every Friday, sometimes soap, tea, razor blades, etc.

Sure I have heat in my hotel room. A coal fire is built every afternoon in such a way as to keep the room very warm and comfortable until midnight, except on some rare occasions when it is terribly cold outside it gets a little cold in here. Every morning at 7:30 we are brought two buckets of hot water. We have running cold water.

Our per diem has been raised, according to grade. I now get 1750 zlotys per day. I really can't give you a good explanation of all this money stuff, you know. As I get it, there is no official exchange rate yet established. But in a store an American dollar is worth 450 to 600 zlotys. It varies from day today, usually is around 500. An English pound ($4.30) is worth 600 zlotys. You realize of course that we get paid in zlotys only, never in dollars. It's all sort of illegal I guess, but I don't understand quite how. And there is practically no cover up on it. The American Embassy pays its drivers in dollars, fifty a month, which converted into zlotys is more than the president gets, about twice as much. I am told. Cameras have gone up considerably since I've been here. But I'm going to get my automatic Rollei soon, for seventy five or eighty bucks. Les Atkins will lend me the needed fifteen or twenty five, and you can send him a check when he gets home.

Lights don't go out at a certain hour, no. Whaddya think? Boys Camp? Of course I eat at any restaurant I choose.

Since my last letter I've undergone some pretty radical changes in my attitude toward my job, and swung back and forth a little. All this past week I spent in Shaw Jones dark room. Developed everything, then made three contact prints of everything. A hell of a lot of work, and a hell of a lot of prints. And when I got all through I realized that I had very little that UNRRA wanted. I am perhaps being a little silly in expecting that they should want the kind of pictures Roy used to want. Unfortunately, although I can make lots of nice pictures of Polish windmills and gravestones, I'm not too brilliant at concise twenty picture sequences showing UNRRA at work. I'd been thinking I'd send all this extra stuff– the non-UNRRA stuff, which so far is about 75% of what I've shot, straight to Washington, in hopes it would get used there. But now I kind of doubt that I should, or that much would ever happen to it there. I'm kind of stuck for knowing what to do. For one thing, I'm going out much harder to try to produce the kind of stuff Redfern wants, and it will be quite a job for me. I'm pretty inadequate at gathering facts, sensing stories, etc. I'm trained to work only one way, really. That's why I'd be so happy if I could wander Poland a la Montana. But I absolutely can not. So I'll buckle down and try to get a lot of good fake stories. My co-worker hasn't yet arrived. With him this will maybe get a lot easier. I'll continue to make as many good pictures, my kind, as I can, as often as I can get the car to stop. But I'm not sure what to do with them. Maybe I'll just consider them as all my personal property, acquired incidentally while doing UNRRA jobs, and bring them home for Paul Vanderbilt to file. Or maybe I will go all out trying to place stuff myself, from here. I've told Redfern about my plan to get a story in a photographic magazine, and he says OK. After my next trip I'm going to send you a bunch of negatives. Honest to god I don't know whether they are any good or not. I just can't tell. At first as negatives they make me happy, but as contact prints they're pretty sad. They will be general Polish stuff–Warsaw, country, villages, people, etc. No story or sequence. Just try to get them published as a purely photographic business, and make some favorable references to UNRRA, and mention that I am working for them. You can prepare a thing like that, can't you? Get Rosskam's[14] or Delano's help on selection of negatives.

Now another thing. I got a long letter from Lew the other day, and he's quite serious that I should go to work for them. Says he has cabled New York to that effect. And he outlines 10 stories I should do in Poland and send to him fast. Then I should go to Berlin and work with him. By March he means. I can't possibly leave UNRRA until I've done something real good for them. I don't see that I could morally quit before May. I don't see how I could get these non-UNRRA stories for Lew while I'm working for UNRRA, except slowly and accidentally. And I don't think my old FSA pictures would be of any use to *Life* either. Anyway I'm getting kind of sour on my position, and my inadequacies.

Tomorrow or Wednesday I will go on a three or four day trip south with Les and Dick Baradel, photographing medical supplies in use. I arranged this myself with Les, and Redfern's not too happy about it. Doesn't like other people arranging things.

Crowd surrounding UNRRA bulldozer in inauguration ceremony (UNRRA 4614)

About fourteen of us last night had a wonderful song fest in the room next door, Dick Baradel with guitar. We sang everything, and I learned some beautiful Lancashire and Yorkshire songs. There's a very nice young English girl here named Stella, from Lancashire, who reminds me of Tess of the D'Urbervilles.

My dark room is still not ready–no work bench–and by now so many people are using it for bathing that I would have an awful job trying to convince them that it was installed for me personally, as a dark room.

Love
John

———

Wed. Feb. 27

Dear Far Away Blues:–

I had three letters from you today, after a considerable absence. Your latest was written February 16. I guess I haven't written you for some time. I've been out of town with Les Atkins and Dick Baradel since a week ago this morning, got back last night. Spent two nights in Lodz (pronounced WOOTCH), Katowice, and Krakow.

Each of your letters asks shall you send me money. Answer is invariably yes. Over a period of four or five letters I'd like to work up to 40 or 50 dollars again. I have no dollars now. I spent $65 for an automatic Rolleiflex, $50 I had, $10 you sent me and $5 I bought from Les with zlotys. Only today I signed a paper having my $25 field allowance transferred back to you–so you will get that starting February.

Thank you for the picture, but I don't like it much. It's not the kind I can show people. Brian is OK, but neither you nor Ann look like yourselves. I wish you'd try again.

Have I told you how we are all set up in housekeeping here, with hot plate, dishes and pots, eggs, ham, tea, coffee–we eat lots of meals here. And last night 15 people were in for tea and song. Dick Baradel and his guitar, me and my recorder, four feet long, bought in Lodz, not so hot, and me and my chromatic Hohner mouth organ, bought in Katowice, and my two small Hohner mouth organs bought in Krakow. I don't seem to be able to do much with the mouth organ, so I think I will send the chromatic job, with some other things, back via Les, for you to give Jack Delano. I will maybe buy another one before I leave, as they are quite cheap.

———

Saturday, March 2

Dear Penny–

Haven't had a chance to write, but anyway no plane has gone since. I think they go on Tuesdays. I've been in the dark room almost all the time since I got back. I now have my own place on the 1st floor of this hotel, and it's quite OK except for numerous inconveniences. It's a long walk down and up, and people living down there get quite mad because I don't let them have baths. So I have to from time to time. Then they build a coal fire in the bathroom to heat the water, which makes things quite messy. Tomorrow night my trunk from the Liberty Warehouse in NY will arrive. This morning I bought a very nice contact printer. So I'm pretty well all set. It's fun having your own dark room. I must have one when I get back.

Les Atkins got orders to go to Hungary this morning. So I guess he won't get home as soon as he figured, and I probably won't be able to send anything via him.

This trip I was on was quite wonderful. A girl from the Repatriation Ministry accompanied us, and that is the story we followed. It was extremely interesting, in fact without a doubt the best thing I've ever had to photograph. We visited camps and hostels of people coming back from the "so called lost territories" as we say here. And I visited three trains of people on their way from the east to the west. One of the trains was people who'd been in Siberia all during the war. The trains were 50 or 60 box cars, 24–30 people living in each one with their furniture, cattle, horses, etc. It takes three weeks for one of them to get across Poland. Some awfully miserable sights, starved looking people, kids without shoes, women wrapped up in old sacks. On one train were six box cars of Jews, who looked more miserable than anyone else. They are segregated of course.

This Jewish thing here is so far beyond my understanding that it is incomprehensible. I have listened to, from Poles, some anti-Jew talk that really far surpasses anything you've ever heard: that Hitler had done one great thing in the world, and how unfortunate he hadn't the chance to finish off the remaining 80,000 Jews–this is said not jokingly or smirkingly, but dead seriously by Poles who fought in the insurrection, who suffered under Hitler, were in concentration camps themselves.

It would be very easy to get general and hate all Poles. But I really like them a lot, as people. I've grown quite tolerant of their anti-Russian sentiments–they are so understandable. Now I don't mean I've become anti-Russian, but I've seen a lot of things now which give me the basis for knowing how Poles feel. They are such damn good people, out in the country, and so very musical. They love Russian songs, but always apologize when they sing one.

I went through one experience, on a train, which I think was about the most moving of my life. It's a cold raw winter morning, see, and this train has stopped for a few hours or a few days, no one knows which, in the rail road yards at Katowice. Our party of course is an object of very great curiosity. We are followed by a crowd of a couple of hundred where ever we go.

I got into a box car where people were living with horses, and saw a guitar on the wall. I pointed to it and indicated I'd like to have someone play while I made a picture. A young girl got it down, and four or five people sang a very stirring Polish national anthem. Then the whole car joined in the singing, and women had tears running down their faces, and the crowd gathered outside the car was actually sobbing–Jesus that was really something– people coming back to their own country after six years in Siberia, and in the miserable condition they were, singing this song–I couldn't keep tears out of my eyes, and I certainly couldn't do the scene photographic justice.

Then later on another train a man who said he was the chief–I guess the leading farmer in the village from which they came, invited me and Les down to his car for a drink–Les and I, the man and his wife and about 4 other inhabitants killed a bottle of bimba with one glass passing from hand to hand. Then they fed us–black moldy bread with pieces of fat meat on it–the meat was so smelly and rancid that I came very near vomiting when I bravely put my teeth into it for a try. We couldn't not eat it, of course, so I nibbled around the bread and gradually got all the meat into my pocket. That pocket still smells foul.

Krakow was one of the most marvelous places I've ever been–a real medieval looking city, not at all destroyed–it was the capital under the Germans–full of ancient churches and castles, and a very wonderful old market place with all kinds of strange beautiful things in it.

It was in Krakow that Dick Baradel bought a new, spanking new automatic Rollei for $30. Mine is definitely a banged up camera for $65. Prices are high in Warsaw. But if I could get ahold of some money quick I think it would be a good idea for me to add $35 to that 65 and exchange my Rollei for a new one.

In Krakow I met Germaine Kanova who had just arrived. She is something of a wonderful woman. French, born of Czech parents, she is now a British subject, and on assignment for *Parade*–you know US *Parade*. She had come across Europe on some of UNRRA's new locomotives for Poland, and is here now to do several Polish stories for *Parade, Life*, and Pix (agency). She studied photography in Vienna with Marion Post[15] and knew her quite well. She is 42 years old. She studied piano in Paris where her teacher's name was Debussy, and you ought to hear her play–real wonderful–strong like a man. She got to Warsaw last night and will be here for a few weeks. I'm letting her use my dark room. I remember some of her pictures in *Life*.

Last night was a reception, for new UNRRA people to meet old UNRRA people. The staff must have more than doubled since I arrived here. I had my first long serious talk with Drury last night, but I can't remember what we could have been talking about–though everyone tells me we talked for half an hour. I got pretty vodkad up last night.

Four Norwegian girls have arrived here. They are nice. But somehow I can't take Norwegians the same as I take other people. They are more foreign to me than any other branch of the family. We have a couple of fine Irishmen, some Scots, Australians, New Zealanders, Czechs. Lots of Swedes in town, non-UNRRA. It's very international, when a lot of us get together and sing from our national countries. Really great fun, this life, in a way. This girl Stella Traynor I think I mentioned to you, from Lancashire, is of Polish descent, and is really quite a fine girl.

Sunday night.

As Ever: Today I finished all my developing. There were some great disappointments where my synchronization was out. But on the whole it looks good–certainly it should be some of the best pictures I've ever made. Tomorrow I hope to be able to start printing. We ran into lots of snow on the way south–first real good heavy snow I'd seen in Poland. How I would like to do this country in my own way–again on this trip we couldn't just stop when I saw a picture, and I had to pass by some of the most magnificent landscapes or whatever you call them–snow with little shawled women and aircraft guns, and wonderful skies.

I might go back to Katowice toward the end of this week. Do you find all these places on the map? If you look? I'm often very surprised, like to find that Wroclaw, which I couldn't find anywhere, goes on old maps under the name Breslau, Germany's fifth city.

Walter Yashakowsky has as yet made no appearance whatsoever. No doubt has been assassinated by the security police.

Well, give my regards to everybody. I will be back among you before many more winters. Wonder what the hell I'll do then. I've drawn a lot of pictures for hanging about the room. Let us hear from you.

Yours.
John

———

Stella Traynor

St Patricks Day

Dear Penny:–

It's been a long time since I've written to you; although I've had many letters written out to you in my head, I haven't gotten to writing any of them. I've been getting frequent correspondence from you–about six I think, since last I wrote to you. I went on a trip east, about ten days ago, through the most war devastated areas of Poland–where the heaviest Russian German fighting took place. It's very ruined and raped looking for miles and miles. People living in dug outs, whole towns wiped out. This was a government sponsored trip. A party of about twenty went–Red Cross people, Polish newspaper people, MacClanachan, me, and kid Kanova, of whom I've told you. She is wonderful, really. And a very good photographer. She is coming to New York in a few months. I hope you will get to meet her. We went out one night in a little village with an interpreter, to find night life, and photograph it. We couldn't find much, so we made some, in a restaurant with a piano. Everything was very dark–no lights in this town, no people on the streets, everyone afraid of Russians. But the piano drew in quite a crowd. I danced a szarzod with an old man with a black beard, and it was the best dancing I ever did in my life. We were quartered in an old castle outside the town.

So I will tell you about my accident. When we got back to our castle, in the dark, I slipped and fell down the stone staircase and was knocked out. Concussion I had, they say. I banged the back of my skull awfully. Nothing broke, and there wasn't even a bump, but I bled via the nose for nearly 24 hours, and the bump on the back of my head brought huge purple circles to my eyes which have only now gone away. I spent two days in a little hospital where some lovely nuns took wonderful care of me. Then I came back here and stayed in bed two days. Now I am fully and completely recovered, and it was all very interesting. Don't worry about me. I won't do it again.

Last night about twenty of us celebrated St. Patrick's eve. Our two Irishmen threw the party at the Europeska, Warsaw's swankiest, where they have a really good jazz band–plays like Duke Ellington–in fact uses many of his very arrangements–the Mood, Aunt Tilly–and has a really remarkable trumpet, like Armstrong. We all had a piece of real shamrock to wear which Brian Moore received from Ireland. I had the only St. Patrick's Day card in all of Poland. Polly Brown sent it to me. Brian Moore is a fine fellow–a literary Irishman, and a student of Joyce–also acquainted with Thomas Wolfe and Dos Passos. It was a good night, and we sang lots of Irish songs. We sing a lot here–it's a very good practice. We ought to do that more at home with our friends.

My pictures of the repatriates from the southern trip have been very well received. Everyone likes them. But I'm very afraid they will not be well used. Mr. Redfern is not smart about pictures, and he is the boss. He picks out a dozen and sends them to London. I'm afraid they will die or get lost. And one of them is I think maybe the best picture I ever made—certainly the only great picture I ever made of people. It's a group of about fifteen repatriates, mostly women, some men—looking up at me—no one is smiling, everyone looks right directly at me in a way that could be called accusing, or something. The picture could be called "the eyes of Poland" or something like that. It really is wonderful, and would make a fine full page in Life. It looks like a Dorothea Lange. It was made from that box car where the people were singing—like I told you about [see p. 109].

There are many other fine pictures too—of the Jews, and of children. I hope you'll see them published. I'm collecting quite a pile of negatives which I can only regard as personal. UNRRA has no use for them. I've developed but not yet printed my pictures from the eastern trip. They're OK too.

I received my trunk, and was disappointed to find nothing personal in it whatsoever. I thought I might have stuffed a book or a sweat shirt into it. Several of the bottles of chemicals were broken.

I'm afraid I'll never get the music you say you've sent me. Packages just don't seem to arrive. I also give up on that suit. Wish I had it, and a top coat. My UNRRA great coat is awfully dirty.

I went out the other day with Ana Maria, my best Polish anti-Semitic friend, to look for the Segal family. We went to most of the addresses you sent, and to others which people suggested. They were all empty ruins. The most definite thing we could get was at 7 Orla Street, a woman who had recently returned there from Germany, and was living in a room in that building, remembered the Segal family, and said they were alive, three of them, on Sept. 7, 1944, after the insurrection started, and the Germans took all the people in that building to a town 20 miles west of here. She remembers those people going with them, but didn't see them again and doesn't know what happened to them. Apparently they were passing as non-Jews, because they moved twice after the Germans came, but did not live in the Ghetto. If they were found out to be Jews, she says, they were killed—otherwise they might have gone to Germany, like herself.

We will make some inquiries through a central Jewish committee here, and I'll let you know as soon as I get anything definite.

I would like some good pictures of you and yours. Honestly, I don't have anything to show people. Browns sent me some pictures of the kids in which Ann is at her most neurotic looking—thin, bitten lip. The two pictures I have of Ann are both terrible.

46

John with Ana Maria Dembinska

I received your envelope of clippings. I enjoy those very much, and would welcome more.

Penny, I love you. But I do not love all of your imagery: "over to the bed when you are in it, not asleep but just arrived there yourself, fresh from the tooth paste tube, and waiting anticipatorily." That sounds like an antiseptic couple residing in a model community.

Did I tell you Les has to go to Hungary? He's gone. From London or Paris he will mail you a package, of which the chromatic mouth organ is for Jack, unless you want it. And the other stuff is to be divided among the three of you. It's not much.

Dick Baradel says you do receive packages here—it takes about three months.

I have some very good times here. But I'm really quite tired of this life and would like to quit it. It's impossible to be a free and independent spirit here.

I saw Tito yesterday as he drove through the city.

I went to a couple of dances just before Lent started—students' dances. They danced all night—quite fun. Sort of carnival, before Lent, like in South America. Well.

Love–
John–

———

April 2. night.

Dear Penny:

Just arrived back to Warsaw, an hour ago, after nearly two weeks absence. And find here only one letter from you. Just before I left I received a package of four shirts, mailed Jan 8. The shirts are of very little use, really. Rather worn, etc. That's the only package I've received. Also just before I left I mailed you a bunch of negatives, via Patty Shaw Jones' sister in England. Do hope you've got em, and please advise. Also did you ever get the package sent by Les? I've decided I can learn to play the harmonica—I do pretty well on my little one, so I'm going to get another chromatic.

I'm awfully sorry about the income blank. Thought I'd signed it. But why don't you send me some stamps and money? I want some dollars, understand? They are the only good universal means of exchange. I want $50, in 10's in five letters. Why you are having money trouble beats me, but I guess that's the way you are.

On this trip from which I'm fresh back I went with the Shaw Jones, both of them. We went first to Krakow, three nights there—worked another repatriation story—went to Oswiecem, perhaps known to you as Ausweitz. I don't know how it's spelled, but it was the German's biggest horror camp. We had a long look through it–it's very vast–it held 75,000 people–saw the gas chambers, furnaces, soap factory, etc. Nothing horrible to see, but just looking at the dynamited gas chambers, the electric fences, and barricades you get a strong sense of evil. We were told numerous stories, legends, etc. Part of it is now used as a repatriation camp, and we worked a story around it.

I talked Latin with a priest. Met a big party of Swiss officers and correspondents there, and were invited to their banquet. Charming people. Went to Katowice.

Photographed a train load of *displaced gypsies*, headed for Besarabia. Such wild beautiful people they were–all dirty and barefoot and in bright colors and beads. They have beautiful dark eyes, and are so totally unlike Poles, of course, but it would be hard to imagine how totally unlike until you see a train load of them in the same condition as a train load of Poles. We were really mobbed by the children–as soon as I'd point the camera hundreds of them would come screaming pushing laughing snarling–getting their faces right up to the lens–it was impossible to plan a picture, but I shot a lot, and I think I got some real beauties. I don't think there is much UNRRA to this story–and I'm going to send you some more negatives–gypsy ones. They should be very placeable–excellent angle: Displaced gypsies–no? I hope you get hot on this stuff.

We went on west to Breslau, called Wroclow in Polish. That was the most extremely interesting part of the country yet. The new territories, you know. Still hundreds of thousands of Germans there–they wear white arm bands–even little children. All the towns are very German looking, and quite attractive, although some of them, little villages, are even more destroyed than towns in the east–we stopped in one just absolutely ravished– only Germans were living in it, and it was a pretty sad picture–people looked hungry, and they were such damn good simple ordinary looking people. Lots of German graves with their helmets over the cross. Breslau is like Berlin–its destruction is really more breath taking than Warsaw's because these miles and miles of empty shells stand–it too seemed a beautiful city–more so I think than Warsaw ever was.

I made a few Esso oval shots there for Roy. We got nice rooms in the only hotel–big shots we are–and were warned not to go out on the streets after 6 PM. Hell of a lot of shooting to be heard all night. We had a piano in my room, and Patty played and we drank cherry brandy. Stayed here two nights, but didn't really get a chance to see much of the city because we worked on the repatriation thing a few miles out of town. I want to go back there.

We went to the terminus of these trains coming from the east, and selected a family who we followed thru–on the train, traveling, eating, etc. Arrival at Wroclow, unpacking furniture into a truck, going into town, registering, getting food cards, being deloused,–they stay here in a camp for a few days, get assigned a farm—we faked this, took them out to a farm which was given to another repatriate and photographed them on it. A darned good story, I think. Our family was from Lithuania—the eldest boy played some very nice Lithuanian sounding music on an accordion. From Wroclow we went south and some west. I don't know the German names for these places, but they were some very interesting towns—Nyssa, Kladzko, and Glucholazy, right on the Czech border—which I crossed, needless to say, border crosser that I am.

Here we went to a TB sanitorium a few miles out of town, up in some nice mountains, where the director was a friend of our interpreters. We were invited to spend the night there, and it was exceedingly pleasant. One of these ultra-modern places with swimming pools and great vistas—very Hitleresque, and full of Luxury and German art and books. We had a long pleasant evening in the director's apartment looking at German painting, playing the piano, drinking the director's peach vodka. Made some pictures in the town the next day—it was a very beautiful little place, altogether undamaged and had a huge church like this (rough drawing of a tall steepled church) all plain in front, but with lots of gargoyles around the little low doorway.

From there we went to Katowice, along the Czech border, and these towns were the most picturesque I've seen—very Slavic they seemed—people in bright beautiful clothes, houses all painted bright, barnyards all white washed and brick walled, with big white geese walking around. And a lot of good religious art—shrines and crucifixes, home made.

Then we went back to Krakow, and met by arrangement the Ebishes—we had seen them the week before, and we went with them to Zakopane. They are a couple, friends of a friend of Patty's in London, whom she was supposed to look up. They are Jewish. Polish. Lived in Paris for 20 years, and came back here in 1939 for a visit. He is a painter, and is now Director of Fine Arts at Krakow University. They are very wonderful people. He's about 45, Genu, and is obviously dying—he's got some bad heart disease and is always getting tired and pale. She, Francesca is about 35, and beautiful as hell. They are both merry and happy and witty all the time, very Ernest Hemingway or something. They invited us to spend the weekend at the University's chalet in Zakopane. Which we did.

Zakopane is straight south of Krakow, 80 miles, again on the Czech border which again I crossed. It's smack in the mountains—Carpathians. It's unreal, it is. Just like a Sonja Henie movie. All the men in the village and on the farms in the valley wear tight pants, light colored with flowers embroidered all over them, and embroidered vests, and big hats with ribbons. It was wonderful warm spring and sunny, little lambs jumping around, first real spring I've seen since Montana, and a river ran by right under my window at the chalet. And always you could look up at the mountains where the snow was so bright you couldn't look—really big mountains. We went up to the top of one by cable car—not Genu with the bad heart. About a half hour ride, and pretty fearful, riding over little peaks—you know the kind I mean—high up in the air—on a cable. Up on top was a big ski lodge and hundreds of people skiing—the real Switzerland stuff this was. Here we walked over the ridge which was the Czech border and I had my picture taken with a fine range of Czech mountains in the background. I got a very good sunburn in about three hours up there Sunday afternoon. All we had to eat all weekend was bread, boiled eggs, and boiled milk—in our chalet—all we wanted of these things, but nothing else. The most remarkable part, which I haven't mentioned yet is that our hosts spoke French and Polish only—the Shaw Jones speak French like I do, and Polish much poorer. So we had a hell of a lot of fun just trying to talk to each other, and succeeded very well, even to telling funny stories—some really amazing garbles of English-French-Polish—all in one sentence. When put to it, like that, I get pretty proud of my Polish—I can almost get around with it. We played that three way drawing game evenings.[16] And chess, which I didn't.

Monday we photographed a sanitorium near Zakopane and went back to Krakow, and left this morning for Warsaw. It was one fine trip, and very productive. This idea of two photographers on the same trip is of course pointless—but Redfern approved of it. Neither of us did anything different—we both covered the same things. My pictures this time will have the advantage of going out with a good story, as Patty was with us everywhere, and noted voluminously.

I have a solid week of dark room ahead of me now, and hope I don't have to go out of town before I finish it.

We were out of Warsaw when Hoover was here. I'm not too sad that I missed that assignment.

I've got wind of something pretty wonderful. For 2000 zlotys I can have a weeks trip, conducted, to Moscow, if I can get the proper visa, which there is no reason to think I can't. I have already enough annual leave to take a week off, and I'm going to try to make it about the end of this month, and maybe see the May Day Celebration.

I gather there is anti-Russian feeling growing back home. I don't know anything about the over all picture from here—Persia, Manchuria, etc. But I know conclusively, the more I travel Poland, that I approve of this government, whether it's Russian dominated or not. Even here in Warsaw I hear things so often about what the Russians are doing in other parts of Poland that I begin to believe them—and then I travel around the country and see what a pack of lies I've been swallowing. I'm going to learn Russian. It should be easy, after Polish.

Guess what I'm reading: *Sister Carrie*. I found it in Krakow, and bought it.

You don't much mention your receipt of my letters—I'd like to know if you get them all. Your hesitance in sending me money makes me wonder. Now I haven't written one in two weeks though, so don't think you've lost one. Brian's recent letter was very nice. I will answer it soon. Also received the color photo of Ann. How about others? Hope you get my negatives soon—and write me about them right away—what advice you get, etc. What does anyone think of them. Enclosed photos were made to show you my bad eyes.

Love
John.

PS. You might as well save money and send my letters APO. I get them quick.

——————

Saturday. April 6, 7, or so

Dear PENNY:

I love you. Tomorrow morning I am going on a trip to Konigsberg. You know? East Prussia, it was. I'll be gone about a week I think. Going with MacClanachan. My deputy boss. Don't know if I've told you fully about him. I had wrong first impressions of him which made me think he was all right, in his way, but he's a genuine no good guy, I think. Revising first impressions, Redfern, the boss, is not a bad guy. He is honest, and you can talk to him. But he is stupid, and certainly not a public relations man.

The Shaw Jones are leaving here on April 22. I'll be sorry to see them go.

I've had several letters and clippings from you these past few days. Your last few letters were very nice. Just like one's wife should be. The clippings were good too. Send me some more.

I return your mother's and father's letter: Have I not been appreciating your mother all these years? I think this is a wonderful letter she has written—really documentary of the times, American, etc. About the street car route, and Viola's kid's colds, and the strikes.

I've had a Christmas, Valentine's, St. Patrick's and now an Easter card from Polly. Also a can of condensed coffee I got from her yesterday. Useful stuff, but I'd rather receive tooth paste.

I'll send you some pictures. Save them in People and Things. This is a photo of the Black Madonna in the church at Chestochovic. Very nice, I think. Also an interior of same church. Next comes: Francesca, our host at Zakopane. She's a very nice kid. The man with the balalaika is Genu, her husband, looking like an idiot, which is what he is a very good one of. Then we have me, in Czechoslovakia. That's Poland behind me. A picnic on K rations with the Shaw Jones on our way south. That's me drinking out of the bottle. The girl in the checked skirt is a kid we gave a ride to. Me with my new Rolleiflex. Test shots. Me outside my hotel room in Krakow. J.S. Jones, same. Another picnic on K rations with Francesca and Genu, on our way to Zakopane. Now do you see what everyone looks like?

I got the ten dollars and thank you. I almost needed it.

After I get back from East Prussia I will write you a letter telling you all about Poles and zlotys and UNRRA people, etc. like you suggest I haven't been doing.

So much I hope you've received those negatives. I've got a lot more I'd like to send you when I know you've got those, and when you tell me you think maybe you can place them. Really, I am a good photographer. Yesterday I printed all the stuff from the last trip with Shaw Jones. And they are magnifico. I won't expand. But they are some of the very best pictures I've ever made. I'll have to turn most of them in. But I'm trying to conserve some for my own uses. Because. The other day Redfern showed me a letter from ERO, the London office, commenting on my pix of repatriates. It said—good pictures, but hardly of use to UNRRA—only two of the 64 had any UNRRA angle—an UNRRA official with a flash on his shoulder in the picture—. As far as I can figure it out those pictures which I give them are just lost. They won't be used unless they say UNRRA in block letters. Including my real master shot of those Polish eyes. Redfern "doesn't think" the negatives get to Washington. So it's all very disappointing. But I've now got a couple hundred good negatives to bring home with me. Better than the stuff I sent you, because I've gotten better since then, and more personal, more people. What can I do with them when I get home?

Haven't seen any movies. Never have time.

I'm sorry Penny, about seeming not to answer your letters, or respond to them. I get the very same feeling from you. No reactions, like you say.

Sasza has reappeared at the Kongo. I guess he was ill. I sure wish I had another suit.

I am very interested in these courses you are taking. Picture sequences, etc. My god that is what I can't do well. I just can't waste my time making it be a sequence. I turned all those Brethren and Conspuctions (sic?) over to UNRRA, so I haven't anything from that set to send you. I have however, completely revised my way of working here, and my attitude. The idea of good historical pictures for UNRRA, in the Stryker manner is totally incomprehensible. So from now on, for UNRRA I make only what I think they will use. The others I keep for myself.

I sure don't know anything about pictures of mine that Miss Mary Taylor of Children's Bureau could have ever got a hold of. I don't think Washington has yet received anything except British MP's, railroads, and Brethren's cows.

Picnic with John Shaw Jones, Patty Shaw Jones, and an unknown female

Germaine Kanova. I enclose a picture of her too. Save it for People and Things. This was made on our trip to Pultusk and northeast. She is leaving for London soon, and will probably turn up in US this summer. Look for her. She is really a very nice person.

Last night I made a wonderful drink, with 12 egg yellows and sugar beaten, a half liter of alcohol, and some powdered coffee. Like Zabaglioni, only better.

Warsaw is very nice now these days. Spring and soft. One doesn't wear an overcoat, though I wish I had a top coat.

Also here are two pictures of my friend Stella. Put them in People and Things. She is a very nice girl–English, Lancashire she talks. Polish-Irish is her descent.

I'm getting so I can enjoy myself on the harmonica! I think I could get good, if I had some time.

Well, write me a long letter and tell me all about people and things. How is Feely? I haven't written any letters for a long time, to: Feely, Kennedy, Heard, Stryker, etc. I want to write. Also my mother.

I got the color picture of Ann. Very nice. Where are some more?

Love.
John

Let me know whether you get the three envelopes of this letter all on the same day ––

———

Saturday night. April–13

D.P.:

Where was I? about a week ago, I believe. Sometimes I miss you tremendously and want really with all my heart to be with you to talk to. I wonder how it would go if we tried it.

Last Sunday morning I went on a three day trip with MacClanachan and two correspondents from Berlin, friends of Gittler's. One is a writer, American, Bill Richardson, the other a photographer, British, Leonard McComb. He does assignments for *Life* frequently. We went to Gdansk, and thence to Olstyn in East Prussia, and traveled about East Prussia some. It's terribly devastated. Whole cities look almost totally dead–three or four Germans shuffling along and no other signs of humanity. It was a very interesting and informative trip, but no pictures at all–no time. We went to a repatriation train in Olstyn and McComb worked there for about six hours–I made a few shots, but I'm pretty stale now on repatriation. This guy Richardson was a friend of Thomas Wolfe–he says. They were both quite nice fellows–the photographer reminded me amazingly of John Collier,[17] and you know it isn't usual to have anyone remind you of J.C. He has his same attitudes, airy, abstracted manner, artiness, etc.

Yesterday I went about 30 miles south of here with Larry Allen–do you know of him?–Time or Associated Press–I'm not sure which–and with W.A. White who is here for two weeks–the same White who wrote that book on the Russians. So there is another penetration of the iron curtain of censorship. He reminds me of a Methodist minister from Kansas. But he drinks vodka. So do I. Sometimes there just isn't anything else to do. I'm pretty fed up with everything here, and I'd like to go home and live sanely and quietly and drink two cocktails before dinner like Phil Brown.

I don't feel at all like writing tonight. I mean I feel incapable of telling you everything, the way it is, etc. I don't feel lucid. But I'm writing because I have a free evening.

I wish Lew would come here. I'd like to go away with him. The UNRRA staff must now be about a hundred. And there are thirty more still to come. It's just unbelievably ridiculous. We are no longer the small intimate group we were when I first came. Now there are dozens of people I don't even know. But I'm so damn sick of it. I want to go home or to Paris or Berlin or any place. And I don't want to work for UNRRA again as long as I live.

I received today from you two letters. Your letters are getting very good, I think–or else my interests are changing. Well written, full of flavor. Tell me sometime about the S.O. Company–maybe you have told me in bits and pieces but I've forgotten, and I'd like the whole picture. Who works for Roy? Not Sol at all? Gordon? What and where does Esther do? Who is Sally Forbes? Did Delanos ever get a letter from me?[18]

Your life, as I piece it out of letters, seems quite different from what it used to be. You seem to be going out a lot, having girl friends, etc. It's hard to imagine you bowling though. Your letters make me think you will become a good writer of magazine articles. I'll bet you would do wonders with all the rich material over here which I am wasting and not getting. I will probably come home and find you a successful writing woman, and from then on I will be a washed up bum, and people will wonder why you support me. Or maybe you won't.

There has been no answer yet from that Jewish committee looking up your friend's family, but I will definitely find out everything that can be found out. You asked for the name of the place they went to–PRUSZKOW–but that doesn't mean anything–it was just the gathering point for all people who were going to be sent to Germany or to camps or be killed.

Redfern is leaving in about six weeks. He's not a bad guy at all. MacClanachan is totally and unbelievably incompetent. He writes badly, and he can't do anything that I can see in the way of public relations. An American-Pole, another one, is now due here shortly–he will probably take Redfern's place. I guess I will move to the Polonia, into Shaw Jones' room, but I'm not too happy about it. It's a nice room of course, but my room mate will be Frank Silewsky, an American. From Chicago. Living with Sig has been pretty damn good all told–I don't think anyone else in UNRRA would get on my nerves any less than Sig. But I would like to live alone most of all. However I need Shaw Jones' dark room, so I guess I'll go.

I bought a shirt and a pair of pajamas. 2000 for pajamas. 900 for shirt. The dollar still gets from 5 to 600 zlotys. We get 1750 zlotys a day, per diem–we don't pay hotel bills out of that however. A box of matches or a newspaper costs two. Cup of tea twenty. Coffee forty. Eggs nine each (in a store). Ham and eggs 120. Bottle of vodka 200 (pint). A good dinner 4, 5 or 600 with vodka. but if you have anything at all fancy to drink like slivovicha, or jebroofka, the price can go way up. Nine zlotys an hour is average labor pay. White collar government jobs get 4 to 5000 a month. Only people who work for the government, which is about 1/4 of the total population, get UNRRA food, the idea being that the limited amount of food should be eaten by essential people–railroad workers, factory workers, etc.–all this of course gives rise to the flood of stories about how government officials live off the fat of the land and the fat of UNRRA, while the people starve. I've seen a lot of government people, in traveling around, including big shots, and they sure aren't living off any fat. Like any half baked reporter I think I gave you a lot of wrong impressions when I first came here. The food, after coming from England, was pretty startling, and it still is wonderful, for us rich people, but not quite so lavish–three meatless days a week–none of them Friday–also three ciastka less days. Ciastka is what you call those elaborate and fancy cakes which are really something. Those three banquets I had that day I went out on the government horse farms were really an exception. I've been since fed by the government in several places, and on pretty simple fare. The farms had a lot of food because they were farms, naturally. It probably sounds silly to you, but the fact that there are these wonderful meals in Warsaw really makes it hard to realize that Poland is full of underfed people–even when you know facts. To photograph Poland properly I should go underfed myself for a few months.

Thanks for the $10, and all the fine clippings. I even read the backs of them, every word. I'm anxious for you to get my negatives, and let me know whether you want any more. Love, and I hope I can get back to you and reconstruct our lives pretty soon.

X

Tuesday after Easter

My Dear Wife:

I have been remiss. And So Have You. Haven't had a letter all week last or so far this. My goodness I have been away from you a long time. It's getting so I miss you a lot, and also wonder what another life than this is like. I'm anxious to see how I can fit back into the old New York routine. A few days ago I suggested to Redfern that I'd like to resign. Of course he is resigning in another month, but he came over with that understanding. He's going to the American Embassy. He pointed out that I could not play UNRRA dirty and leave her in Poland with no photographer whatsoever. Which is true, I guess. So in a way it is like a horrible nightmare which I can hardly believe is true but there it is. But I've asked the Shaw Jones, who left Sunday, to look for some down at the heels photographer in London and send him out here, and I think they might find such a person. I'll wait until I hear from them in a few weeks–then I will announce my resignation as of July 1, and they should have a photographer here by then if they want one. Only if Lew comes here, and I'm much hoping he will, and persuades me to join him, I wonder what I'd do then.

Here are some pictures. Two of me. One of me and Warsaw from the roof of the Polonia. The other is at Shaw Jones farewell party in Gertrude Mott's room. The people in it are– Rear: John Shaw Jones, Ana Maria Dembinska, our Polish anti-Semitic friend who went with Les and me on that trip–withal a good sound intelligent girl, Barbara Moberly, from Frederick, Maryland, Stan Pritchard from Northern Ireland. He is a nice guy and is in love with Barbara Moberly. Next row: Doug Cannon, with whom I went to Poznan. He is from California. He's going to marry Gertrude Mott from North Carolina shortly who is not in the picture. She was holding the light for me. Patty Shaw Jones. Nelson from the American Embassy. Gene Hayes, bottom row and a fine man. Ann Rozak, Drury's secretary, McDonald from the American Embassy and Dick Baradel.

I had a nice Good Friday and Easter. Good Friday I went to church. Saturday I went with the Shaw Jones to a driver's house for tea and to a place called Willanov (Villa Nova) where there is an exact replica of Versailles, where some prince used to live. Very interesting and nice. Right on the river. Sunday I also went to church. And Sunday night I went to the Opera, with Stella Traynor and a Polish girl named Helena Jasminska. The opera was *Madame Butterfly,* sung all in Polish, and I think it is a stinky opera.

I went photographing one day last week to an orphanage here in Warsaw, with a girl who said she'd been very anxious to meet me. She is a friend of Arnold Eagle's and she tried to get to meet you a couple of times at Rockefeller Plaza but always missed you.[19] She

Shaw Jones' farewell party *(from left to right, top to bottom):* John Shaw Jones, Ana Maria Dembinska, Barbara Moberly, and Stan Pritchard; Doug Cannon, Patty Shaw Jones, and Nelson (from the embassy); Gene Hayes, Ann Rozak (Drury's secretary), McDonald (from the embassy), and Dick Baradel.

says she is a journalist. And she's on assignment from *Collier's*. She's a good kid, I guess. But My God. Perhaps I can't see her hidden qualities. But I don't see how someone like her could ever write anything good. You, I think, ought to be a real wow of a magazine article writer. And after you finish your course if you want to come to Europe for *Collier's* I will gladly stay home to give the children a father's guidance, and that is no joke. I wish you would do that, or something like that.

One of the kids at the orphanage sang for us, and it was very beautiful and touching. Something about kids being orphans, having their parents killed by Germans or sent away, and still being just like other kids is very touching. One boy whose picture I made I met today in the street—he ran up to me pointing and jabbering in Polish "pan pan, fotografa" so I brought him up to my room and gave him his picture and a milky way bar out of my K ration.

Germaine Kanova is leaving tomorrow. I had dinner with her last night. I hope very much she gets to New York, and you see her. She is a damn fine woman, and I'd like you to hear her play the piano.

This guy Brian Moore is becoming my fastest friend. He is very unpopular here on the mission as he is rude and impolite to people. He is really and truly a poet, and a literary man, but not a mild or sickly one. I like him a lot—I wish I could get him to work with me. He is some very low grade sort of clerk having to do with ship arrivals.

I am now moved to the Shaw Jones' room in the Polonia, and it is quite wonderful to be living in this unaccustomed luxury. It is a large room, quite nicely furnished, a balcony, and a huge bathroom which I've been enjoying tremendously today setting up as my own personal dark room. Also I can take baths. My room mate is not, as I think I wrote you last he would be, Frank Silewski. He is Ed Wrobewski—an American, about 55, from Detroit—Hamtramack. A big shot on the mission—in charge of observation of distribution or something very much like that. He's a lawyer from Hamtramack. A typical UNRRA error, I think. Of course he's anti-Russian. Last night was the first night he's stayed with me, and I sounded him out. He's also anti-Negro and anti-Jew in his subtle way. But I'm not going to let him get on me emotionally. I'll just understand him. He is really a very pleasant guy, and I judge extremely easy to get along with. He is gone now for a week. He travels a good bit, so that's good. Today having this whole large room and bath to myself has really been sort of heaven.

I read *A Tree Grows in Brooklyn*, borrowed it from Baradel. I was greatly disappointed in it. I didn't expect great literature. But you told me it was something I should read, it would get me, I think you said. It didn't get me. I think it was simple, and not pretentious, but just so ordinary a biography, and no fire, or poetry, or thought.

I hope you'll have had a chance to go to Washington to look at the UNRRA files on Poland, if any. Did you ever get my negatives?

LOVE!
John

――――

Saturday. 4 of May

Dear Penny V.: –

Thank you for that fine long letter written April 15th which I received last Sunday just before I left on a very good trip from which I returned at 1 AM this morning, and for the ten bucks.

It's getting so I am extremely anxious to get back to the US and you and the small ones. Even though I have been having some really wonderful experiences the past few days.

Nothing has happened yet on that trip to Moscow. I'm still hoping however.

I haven't sent Edie Atkins those prints yet. It's hard to send things. Yes, Les got a good camera–an Ikoflex. And I guarantee you he didn't write any letters during that trip we made together. There's little time for letter writing in Warsaw, but none at all when traveling. Really. Does Edie pay duty on these fabulous gifts Les sends her? I have a few small items for you, not much, but I thought I'd carry them home in person.

I hope you have some negatives by now. There are many more I hope I can load off on you and get distributed. Much better ones. I got a letter last week from the Curtis Publishing Co. re: their new picture magazine, and they say Ed Steichen suggested me to do things for them in Poland, and they want to know if doing some assignments for them here would interfere with my regular UNRRA work. I haven't answered yet.

Also I had a visit from the correspondent from *Town and Country*, who picked out some pictures he wants from my contacts. Most of the negatives have been sent away to some desk drawer in London, but I'm going to maybe give him some of the negatives I have, and hope they will somehow or other find their way into publication.

I'm quite disappointed of your account of my pictures as seen at the UNRRA office. They certainly should have had more by April. That Gdynia cattle stuff was no good whatsoever and I'm sorry you saw it. I made all those boys under the Polish sign because Gene Hayes wanted me to–for their hometown newspapers. No repatriates? The children in the hospital were sent out the same time the repatriates were. Haven't they got any system yet, of 8 X 10 file prints for everything?[20]

Have taxes been reduced, and are you getting a bigger paycheck now? Have you started to receive my field allowance yet? Should be with February. January and December I drew. I wish it would be possible to have four or five hundred bucks on tap when I get home so I wouldn't have to go to work right away if I didn't want to, or couldn't find a job.

I'm glad you saw that Warsaw exhibit. The photographer you mention, Zofia something, is a friend of Ana Maria Dembinska, of whom I've no doubt told you. She, the photographer, is now traveling in Europe for the government. Will be back in another month, and I will make her acquaintance.

I'm getting a new suit. Not just having a suit made, I'm having the cloth woven first, under my personal direction. Then I'll have a suit made made.[21] It will cost about 26,000. I have about 15,000 saved up, and will be able to lay aside the rest in a few weeks. The American dollar has dropped in value to about 300, and will stay there I guess. I guess it's really wrong to deal in them. The only use I've made of them is the $65 I paid for my Rolleiflex. I won't use the two tens I now have, but if I receive a few more it will be all right, because I might need a little dough when I give up my all here and try to find a cattle boat to come home on.

Germaine Kanova left a week ago or so. I went to dinner with her on her last night, at the Kongo, where Sasza is, and she had a lot of Army-Navy "Hit Kits"–popular songs, which Sasza is now learning. She played the piano, and we all had a very fine time. We ran into a party of Bulgarians who were here to sign a treaty of trade or something, and they took us all to their rooms and gave us Bulgarian wine. A girl, the only member of her party who spoke English, pleaded with me: "Why you do not recognize us? We are a good government." She really had me. I didn't know we don't recognize Bulgaria, did you? So no UNRRA there. They were very nice people–kind of Greek looking. Wrobleski was away, and Sasza spent the night with me that night.

Have I told you all this before? One day last week I went out to a sort of soup kitchen where the extremely poor are fed free. And I got my first good pictures of *really* hungry looking people. Redfern was very pleased with them. I received a package of *NY Times* and a *Sunday PM* from you, and I'm very glad to get them.

Now I must tell you of the trip I've just finished, on which some amazing things happened. I left Sunday noon, on another of these UNRRA press tours, on which I have great difficulty working. Two cars–Me, and MacClannachan and an UNRRA interpreter, two government officials and a Scotch girl, Mary Kavanaugh, representing Glasgow papers, engaged to a Pole in Scotland, and very anti. And an American from the *Hartford Courant.* Very American, and quite stupid. Nice guy however. I used to think a correspondent in a foreign country had to be a brilliant and remarkable person.

We went to Kielce, about 250 KM straight south of here. The center of a great battle area where the Germans held for several months. Devastated area they always say here, like Farm Security's "rural problem areas." This is sure devastated. Just torn up, with miles of ugly looking holes and barbed wire and wrecked tanks scattered around a really beautiful countryside–in the Spring. First night we had dinner and a conference with the Governor of the district–and the chief of the security police. The governor was a real PPR (communist), the first genuine one I've met among big shots. He was very young and energetic, and frank as hell. He made the Scotch lass look pretty silly to me, but I guess she didn't think she looked silly. The next two days, with some more local officials we picked up, we toured that area, and saw how badly off the people are. They live in shacks and dugouts near their destroyed barns and houses. They eat potatoes, and absolutely nothing else but potatoes. They have children, and tell you they had milk last summer, or they had bread three months ago. The women often start to cry when they are being questioned. The fields are still mined, and sometimes when they try to plow them up to put in some more potatoes they get blown up. A woman showed us a piece of a belt which she said was all she could find of her husband. It was pretty miserable, and I got some good pictures. But pictures of this sort of thing are awfully hard to get. Tuesday night Mac and the party went back to Warsaw and left me in Radom, where I was met by Ana Maria Dembinska–she's an interpreter and protocol person for one of the Ministries–and Kit Barker, a Canadian girl, Redfern's new secretary of whom he's trying to make a writer. She's a nice kid, but probably won't make a writer. And a very nice driver. And an open jeep–in which I got a good sunburn, and very dirty. Wednesday was May Day. In Warsaw big preparations and posters had been going on all week, and in Radom, or any of the larger towns we went through, there were parades and bands all day long. But mainly I missed that, as it doesn't happen in the country. I'm sorry I wasn't in Warsaw to see it, but on the other hand I got something I'd have missed otherwise. The day before all through the country I'd noticed little kids walking down the roads with bunches of flowers, and seen them in the woods and fields picking them. Toward evening they were decorating all the roadside shrines of the Virgin Mary with them–first of May being given over to her as well as to Labor. It was a very beautiful peaceful sight–sun low, people coming home, driving cows home, kids decorating shrines and statues. There are shrines all over this country–not just Mary, but numerous other people. Perhaps it's hard for you to understand how I talk about battle scars on the land and starving people, and then about the beautiful countryside and peaceful villages. It's really like that though. For one thing some of the countryside here is as nice as any I've ever seen, and the villages, when they aren't destroyed, and even when they are partially destroyed, are very old and pleasant, bucolic, dignified, etc. And little kids who only eat potatoes even still look good—they are pretty. They get lots of sun out in the country.

On Wednesday we started very early, and with more freedom than I've hitherto enjoyed we drove around the countryside, stopping whenever I wanted to, and visiting many very hungry families and destroyed villages, and I got some fine pictures. We were working east, toward the Vistula, over terribly rough roads. We planned to go to Lublin for the night—and about five miles from the bridge, across the river to another district, we stopped to make pictures in a town when we were all arrested by a soldier who said he had orders to stop for questioning anyone going through that town in a car, motorcycle or bicycle. We were taken to a smelly little building where the commanding officer, a lieutenant, was quite intoxicated from May Day celebration. This was about three o'clock. We argued until five—it was all sort of pleasant—lots of humor thrown in, but we were really in it. They wouldn't accept our stories of who we were—there were no telephones, and they wanted to keep us there while they took our jeep to a place eighty miles away to find out about us. We finally got them agreeable to letting us go with them—four of them and four of us. The jeep had been pretty tight before with just four and all our baggage and cans of petrol. Now we drove eighty miles over the bumpiest damn road in the world. They were all armed, and brought along in addition a machine gun with several feet of ammunition [drawing of a row of bullets] like that you know, which kept falling on my lap. But it was all very friendly, and we made jokes, and even really enjoyed the trip, except it was uncomfortable. And after the first hour the drunken lieutenant decided that Ana Maria and I should not speak to each other in English. Then we got to Kosciency where we were taken over by a major, a very nice polite gentleman, who questioned and listened to us. A Russian officer sat in the room all the time but didn't talk—just observed in an ominous way. And it was all explained to us. We had wandered into an area where there were known to be bandits in the woods—bandits means robbers, AK army, General Anders men, or patriots, according to how you look at it, but they do rob, murder and set fire to villages, and I've no doubt they were in the section we got into. They were starting a real intensive campaign to get them, or at least this particular gang. So everyone passing through was to be apprehended, as they usually dress as Russian soldiers or Polish soldiers, but they might be dressing as UNRRA this trip. On our way to Kosiency we passed only one vehicle—a man on a motorbike who went right by us. They hollered at him and then shot several times in the air until he turned around and came back. Then the lieutenant took his motor bike and put him on the hood of the jeep and we proceeded. The major was terribly sorry we had been inconvenienced, etc. but told us it was absolutely necessary, and was pretty sensible about it all, I thought. The lieutenant was given ten days in the jug for being drunk on duty. I was very sorry because he was a nice fellow, and was very proud of how he was doing his duty. Anyway, I agree with the whole thing that happened–that is I think that is how it should be done if they've got some bandits to clean up. But this is typical of the incidents which British and Americans, UNRRA and correspondents, use to say there is a reign of terror here, and no personal liberty. And there are a hundred different stories as to who the bandits are. I think they are no doubt quite diverse, many being real bandits– criminals, non-political. And I also think there is an organized anti-government gang working with them.

We stayed that night in Kosiency, and I got bitten all to hell, but got some lovely market day pictures next morning. Then we went back toward Lublin again, on a slightly different route, stopping for pictures in peasants' homes. This Polish peasant is really a guy all by himself–a really wonderful manner–not the servile serf like I'd always thought, but a fine proud polite man of the land, with honest to god dignity–it's the only time I've ever been able to use that word. In the towns people crowd around the car, hundreds of them, stare at us, say how wonderful Americans are, ask if we are bringing them food, complain of their troubles, etc.–but in the real peasant villages and out on farms it is entirely different. They treat us as equals, they God Bless Us in a very nice way, they say we honor them by coming into their homes, etc. I don't know if I make that clear–not servile–like if I make a picture in the very poorest of shacks where a man lives with eight children on the land he used to farm–I say thank you, and he says O no, it is you who must be thanked for paying us the honor to stop here and make a picture. To offer money to these poorest people on earth would be impossible. They would be offended, and would not take it. I've been able to pass out some K rations to people like that, but money never. One most beautiful old couple who had a cow which they hid from the Germans invited us in for some milk. There were children all around who hadn't had milk for months. But it was not possible to refuse the invitation. We had two glasses of milk each, and they cut slabs off their loaf of bread made of potatoes and flour, and I'm sure that that loaf of bread was their most valuable possession next to their cow. They were damn wonderful people.

Well then. On Thursday, we are still heading for Lublin. We have crossed the river. And about 4:30 we see a big column of smoke off ahead, like a burning oil well. When we get to it we see it's a village on fire. I wish I could describe this to you but I know I never can. Nothing before has ever torn me up inside like this, and made me so goddam confused as to what I believe in if anything. This was the 2nd of May, and on the east side of the Vistula where not much war damage was, and this was a village of 300 houses which had not been damaged at all. It was beautiful country, and afternoon on a beautiful day, and all the fields around had been planted, wheat was growing up nicely, there were flowers on shrines all along the road, and you got the feeling of the month of May, and the sort of beauty of the normal way of life of a place like this. And even when I got there and saw that the place was burning up I couldn't get it. You read that a village burned down or there was a war, or you see a picture of it, but Christ when you really see that happen.

I went down into a big field at the edge like this. [Drawing] Those are houses, wood with thatched roofs, on the right it's the fire just moving straight thru the town with a slight wind. The x's are the people out in the field running back and forth to drag out more clothes or household goods or pigs etc before the fire gets to their place. On this wonderful May day with good looking crops all around and up on hills, there are a couple hundred people in a big field watching their houses and barns and feed and everything they own burn down. Everyone keeps running back to drag out something more. The pitiful crying of some of the women, and the men with tears on their faces standing there watching as the fire hits their house–they say "that is every thing I have" and little kids about four just stand by the salvaged stuff and watch without crying, kids about eight are sobbing hysterically, a woman puts a little three year old down on a trunk she has dragged out and then runs back to get more, and the kid climbs down and runs around the field, then the woman comes back and cries for her baby–pigs are terrible in fires and won't stay where they are put, everybody's pigs get mixed up and people struggle with them and they squeal and resist and run back into the fire. These poor goddam people who got through a war without being killed, and who still have houses and fields, and it's May, and they're out there watching the places they've lived in all their lives burn up–old sick women being carried out–I helped carry out an old woman who probably hadn't been out of the house for years–her stench was really horrible and she was shaking and praying–but mostly it's all normal people, perhaps a little more emotional than Americans in that they cry more readily and fall down on their knees to pray–I can't tell you about it Penny. It probably just sounds like a fire to you. But I can't think about it with any quietness.

When I was there in that field I couldn't keep tears away no matter what I was doing. I stayed for two hours and watched the fire go entirely through the side of town I was on. People would keep working on bringing out things and not cry or be emotional until the fire actually got to their house, which it was most evidently going to do all along. Then they would break down and weep watching their own place go up.

The big church of course up on the hill was safe all the time. [Another drawing] That kind, looking down on the town. You would speculate as to which areas would get it and which might escape but you knew it couldn't hit the church.

Men would run into barns to drag out wagons and things at the last moment, just as the fire was starting at one end. I saw two men run into a barn, two men in white shirts, the

Fire in the village of Wawolnica, May 2, 1946 (UNRRA 4490)

barn was already burning at one end–I was far away and could see, I don't know whether they knew or not–I thought should I holler out to them not to, or run up there, or would they come out–and then the fire just rushed across that barn with a little increase of wind, and the two men in white shirts never came out. I wish there was a word I could use to tell you about this but there isn't. And the helplessness and stupidity of myself.

A man loaded his wagon with goods and the horse brought it out of the barn, then the horse broke and ran away, and the man and woman tried to push it and it wouldn't move at all–they shouted to me, in a tone I'll never forget and all I did was walk away. I couldn't push the wagon either.

I went down into the field with my camera, and made some pictures at first–long shots, of people all over the field with the burning village in the background, long shots of the fire, and a few close ups of women dragging pigs. But I'm not a Weegee. I couldn't possibly go up to the people I saw and make pictures of them. I did one, a little girl whose face is really in my mind forever. About eight years old, she was sitting on some pillows, crying, holding on her lap a baby–I went up very close to her and photographed her face–then she stopped crying and said something Polish which I didn't understand and smiled a most beautiful smile. Well we went to Lublin that night. It's a very nice city. Next day we went south a bit, worked up the river, same stuff, and came back to the burned town about 5:30. Less of it had burned than I'd thought would be. About 1/3 still stood. We stopped in the square and people gathered around us and told us many stories–we walked around town and heard more, and talked to some soldiers and heard more. I don't know. The day before I never thought but what the fire was a fire, an accident. Now I know it wasn't an accident, but I don't know what's the answer. Bandits did it, secret police did it, soldiers did it–etc. There was evidently some fighting between soldiers and supposed bandits who had taken refuge in the town. And it mostly hit people who don't know what bandits are. When we got back there the church bell up on the hill was ringing steadily, and a funeral of two coffins was walking out to the cemetery and people were singing funeral songs. It was the same kind of quiet nice May afternoon as the day before, and no one was crying anymore, but people were still living out in the fields and black burnt house frames were all over, and the damn church bell kept ringing. Going to dinner now.

Love
John.

—

Child photographed during fire in Wawolnica (JV 303)

Sunday night 5, May

Dear Penny–

I've spent all day developing, and it's all done. I am very extremely happy with the results. I'm really getting better all the time, and now I'm damn near perfect. Really, I made some wonderful pictures this trip–hungry kids and old women in the Dorothea Lange[22] manner–some most beautiful landscapes, real magazine cover stuff. And the fire pictures look sort of terrific–long shots, very sharp and contrasty–beautiful light, smoke and fire in background, daisies all over the field, and little figures of people in tragic poses. I'm beginning to feel that I've done, or am doing a pretty fine complete job of Poland–from a variety of angles–if I could just get it all together some place, sometime.

   Did I tell you that I told Redfern I would like to resign on July 1? I did.

   I've got bugs or something and I am too itchy and sleepy to write further.

                                  Love anyway,
                                  John.

That's Ana Maria in glasses talking to the man in the fur cap.

━━━━━

Tuesday–May 14

Dear Penny:–

I've sure been away a long time. Can't remember when I wrote you last. Anyway in the mean time I've been up to Gdansk and back. By air, 1 hour and 20 minutes. Lots of fun, this Polish air travel. They fly very low and you see everything. Saw a huge flood up near Gdansk, miles of villages and farms under water. Met a very nice stewardess for the Polish Airlines, and took her picture. In Poland the air stewardesses are known as "ripskies."

━━━━━

Wednesday–May 15.

Got interrupted there. Here I am back, next day. Last night I went to a really wonderful cinema program–three full hours, called 50 years of the French Film. From early funny

70

stuff, thru Rene Clair, Raimu, Gabin, up to the fine shots of the Paris insurrection. Very well edited—no whole movies, but sequences out of all the great ones.

———

Saturday. May 18. 10 AM.

Just to let you know I'm still thinking of you. I can't possibly write now though. But I'm definitely coming home on the first of July and I'm going to stay there always. I love you. Don't seem to be getting much mail from you lately.

Saturday May 18. 5 PM

It's raining hard now. I don't feel too well today. Must be something I ate. Joke. I don't feel much like writing to you.

Tomorrow is my birthday. And a Polish girl who works for Sig, is having a big party, forty people. But I don't think it's for my birthday.

Last Thursday was Sig's birthday, and two Norwegian girls had a very nice warm friendly little party for him, about ten of us, and we all sang and toasted, and it was a good evening. I gave Sig as a birthday gift one of my ties which he used to borrow a lot.

I'm very nearly out of pencil. Down to about two inches on this one. Then how will I write to you?

You said I never write anything about Sig any more. Here's what happened. Although we never stopped being very good friends, we got so we practically never saw each other. Sig fell into a condition of love, with Ossa, one of the Norwegian girls, and he spent all of his time, every minute of it with her. He's actually going to marry her. Of course once every two or three weeks he would not see her and we would sit drinking all night in our room talking over old times.

Last night I went to a reception at the Russian embassy, with Ana Maria Dembinska. She is probably my best friend here, because she is smart. Intelligent. She is about 35 years old, and extremely non-beautiful. Then my other friend is Stella Traynor. I've told you about her. She is not so smart. But she is a *good kid*. Really good, so you must get no incorrect ideas. She is my partner at parties. Then there is Brian Moore, he's a man whom I see a great deal and have talks and meals with. He knows all the modern poets by heart, and is a real authority on Joyce, and speaks with a beautiful Irish talk, full of the old funny twistings of sentences. Since the Shaw Jones left, that about rounds up the people who form my "intimate circle." Was it something like that you wanted to know? There are now 130 non-Polish people working for UNRRA.

I'm afraid that box of negatives must have been lost if you haven't got it yet. It's probably just as well, as I'd probably been over rating them. I must say I was rather disappointed in your reaction to those few contacts I sent you. Yes, definitely, the one I regarded as a prize was among them. All the people looking up. But I see so few other photographs now a days I guess it's easy to be wrong. What does anyone else think of them? There's been a couple of references lately in letters both from London and from Washington, to how my pictures are very good.

I'm sure anxious to get back to N.Y. And it looks like there'll be no hitches to my leaving July 1st. Redfern leaves at the end of this month, and I'm very sorry. I've come to like him. Can't seem to flow. So I'll go.

All of my love–
Jno.

Let's go for a long automobile trip in July and August–Dakotas and Montana–Washington, Oregon, California, Mexico and Texas––

—————

Friday. May 24–

My dear Wife:––

Time marches on. Gettin on six months since I seen you. Had two letters and some clippings from you since last I wrote. That Pageant article. Very delightful to see two of my favorite pictures used. Silly vague article though, don't you think?

Sunday I'm going to Katowice with Ana Maria Dembinska. Photograph an arriving railroad locomotive and train, and go into the coal mines, and photograph. Also, maybe the salt mines near Krakow. Dembinska has lost her job at the Ministry. It's a long story and I will tell you about it when I see you, but I carry a burden of responsibility in the matter. It's because she took me to that reception at the Russian Embassy which was supposed to have been very private.

Every time I get your letter I quick scan it to see if you got those negatives. And you haven't. It's a pity that they should be lost. There were good ones.

Sunday I heard a concert, Henryk Stampuck, who played all Chopin. They tell me he's the Chopin man of all times, so I agree. He was very good.

Ana Maria Dembinska

I've been making more pictures lately. All good ones. I've never before in my life felt that I was such a good photographer like I feel now. I think it's because I'm always developing stuff right after I make it. It gives you sureness.

Yesterday a man known as Victor Perry or Victor Alexandrow called on me. He is the author of a book called *Journey from Chaos*. Ever hear of it? He gave me a note to his publisher so I can get a free copy when I go home. He was quite ecstatic about my pictures, so of course he was a very nice and intelligent fellow. I *gave* him about *sixty* negatives, of my personal horde. He will take them to Paris, get them printed, and then they will be published, he says, in Swiss, French, and US magazines, with a credit line, and then he will send me a check, and mail back (to New York) all the negatives not used. I don't altogether believe him. I mainly hope that I get my negatives back sometime. That was probably a foolish thing to have done. The lot to you lost in the mail, another lot given to a strange man, and the rest lying unused in desk drawers. But I don't know what else to do with them.

Victor is on the staff, I believe, of *Reader's Scope*. In the fall he plans a three months tour through the Balkans, and would like me to come with him. Says I should quit UNRRA, go home for a few months, and then meet him in Paris in September. He has a car. And wonderful ideas.

I saw a letter yesterday from Wells, of Washington. My repatriation pictures he says "will be kept as part of the permanent record of UNRRA, but will not be published, as this is an activity that in no way concerns UNRRA"–and their publication "might be resented" or something like that. This sure made me mad. The repatriates here are without doubt of more concern to UNRRA than any other group. This is an awfully cockeyed show of public relations. Lately we've been getting cables from Washington asking for starvation pictures. So Redfern became convinced that we didn't have to have a can of UNRRA beans in each picture, and I went out and got some good ones–those people who eat only potatoes. Now we get a letter from London–"Vachon's photos are excellent as usual, photographically, but of no use to us as a public relations department because there is no UNRRA angle." Isn't this a stupid business? Maybe I could do some good, or fix things up if I got to Washington.

Well I'll see you soon I hope. Is the house clean? Cockroaches? Drapes? Arm chair? Tops of tables etc. orderly? Don't answer. But some day I'm going to have a room of my own.

Love

John

Did I tell you I photographed MIKOLAJCZYK the other day?

▬▬

June 4, Tuesday–

Dear Pennba.–

I'm afraid I've missed the bag again, but I'll write for a new bag. Anyway you sure haven't been doing too well lately. I think it's two weeks since I've heard from ya.

About all I think of nowadays is going home, which is where I'm going for sure, soon.

On Saturday a US Office of Information reading room was opened at the Embassy. And I was sent *to represent Drury* who couldn't be there. It's a very nice library, and I met a lot of people, including Bliss Lane the ambassador, whom I hadn't before. Also it was most gratifying to find numerous little pamphlets, publications of the U.S.O. of I., in French, and Polish, bulging with FSA pix.

I met Homer Bigart, the *NY Herald Tribune* guy. People on short term stays here sure get full of absurd ideas and prejudices. And long termers, like Larry Allen who rarely leaves the Polonia bar, and then writes about what the government is doing 200 miles away–they make me angry. It's easy to see how the world can be full of misinformation when it depends on the kind of correspondents I see.

I've probably said a lot of cockeyed and prejudiced things since I started writing you from Poland, but I've begun to coordinate. I've got confidence now that I really know the score enough not to be misled.

I will tell you of my trip which began a week ago last Sunday. Just Dembinska the driver and I. To Katowice. Stopped en route at Czestochowa–the shrine of Poland–"The Virgin of Czestochowa" you've heard of? Sort of a Lourdes, with some beautiful monumental stations of the cross on the grounds. And that black Madonna picture I sent you. Then all week we stayed in Katowice, and I went down into a couple of coal mines, a very fine experience. I had to dress up like a miner. Three hundred meters straight down, then long meandering walks. It was very hot down there. Some pretty excellent pictures, I think. Mainly I photographed miners and miners' families, but spent some time on UNRRA locomotives and trains. Also made some shots of a Russian troop train carrying soldiers back to Russia from Germany, with lots of German bedroom and living room suites. We got back Friday night, and I finished processing last night.

I hate this business of your sending any of my Standard Oil pix to *US Camera*. It doesn't seem that is how I should be represented if at all in a new edition. Couldn't you pry loose a repatriate negative in UNRRA if it's a rush–or wait until I get home with some negatives, if I have any left.

I wonder if you miss many of my letters–I never can know whether you really know that I went to Gdynia or to Kielce or that I got a new suit or that I haven't had any tooth paste for months, etc. We should have instituted a system of numbering our letters.

What's this I get garbled accounts of about Truman becoming the archest of reactionary backsliders? And have you heard how nicely and smoothly Poland got her loan from Russia after we denied it? I think we are very stupid in our relationship with this country. Now I understand the evil of the so-called career men of the state department. Also, despite the general idolatry of Americans, there is a touch of Anti-Americanism to be felt. And I sure don't like most of the Americans I meet over here.

———

Wednesday–

Quite disappointing, today, to have another plane, and still not a letter out of you. Two big envelopes of clippings however. All very interesting. But my God. They say Poland doesn't have a free press. Nothing could be worse than the dishonest kind of reporting you send me by someone called Pauline Fredrick.

This morning I photographed some of those many thousand eggs hatching on a state farm near here. Kind of good pictures maybe.

I saw that Russian movie *Masquerade* again last night, with Brian Moore. It's still terrific. And I was so happy to be able to understand patches of Russian.

How is little old Brian? I often think of him, and how fine it will be to see him again. I hope he will not have changed much.

I had two letters from Phil Brown this morning. He advises me not to come back to America. The country is going to the dogs he says.

If I should come back to Poland I wonder if you shouldn't come with me, as a writer, and we farm out the children. I will commence to talk up such an idea here, and perhaps in Washington I can fulminate it.

Last night Brian and I went to a circus, after it had closed, and watched various performers practicing climbing up ropes and juggling, etc., and talked Polish to a pretty girl in tights.

I wish I could be in a more direct contact with you. It's so damn long from the time we say something to each other until the other responds to it.

Well I can't think of anything more to say. Seeing I never get any letters from you.

LOVE,
John

June 10

Dear Penny:

Today is Whit Monday, and a legal holiday in Poland. Many of our staff have gone off on weekends etc. Sig and Ossa are taking a week's vacation in Copenhagen, where they will doubtless wed. Moe is in the hospital. Doug Cannon married Gertrude Mott this morning in the courtyard of the Polonia, by a Protestant minister. I was the officiating photographer.

It's now well over three weeks since I've heard from you, so I hope you're all right. I got a Father's Day card from Phil and Polly though.

A few nights ago I went with Brian to see the Russian Ballet from Leningrad–about forty people, all folk dances they did, from different parts of the country. It was really a very exciting business, and the most wonderful colorful costumes. The orchestra was also from Leningrad, and very good–a full big one, including several accordions.

Sasza has gone to sing in Gdynia for the summer. I don't understand why the music you sent never arrived. Or the suit. No one else has lost any packages, and people get books and music all the time. It may be that damn London office not forwarding. Anyway, switch to APO now for everything, that is if you think you might happen to write again. It will probably get forwarded home better that way. Hope I get a letter from you on Wednesday. Anyway I'll be out of stamps soon, and unable to write you.

Love and all best wishes.
John.

Friday–June 14.

Dear Millicent:–[23]

When on Tuesday the American plane came, and on Wednesday the British plane, and still Nothing from you, I said softly and distinctly: "to hell with you." This is really pretty awful. Not even I have ever let you go six weeks without a letter.

Well now I am completely, totally, stuck, trapped, stale, flat, unhappy. I see no possibility of ever making another good picture while I remain in Poland. I am only wasting my time or doing nothing, and I would rather do nothing, so I spend as much time as possible doing that. There not even being anything to read. Even while I walk through Warsaw and see the beggars and one legged old women selling eggs and little boys without hands selling radishes–the crowded street cars and droshkis, and the fallen down buildings behind these things always–I know they are great pictures, and I know I haven't made any of them, and now for sure I won't. I'm a goddam UNRRA man, and I'm rat-like here in my maze wasting and butting my head and drinking vodka and listening to fifth rate pianists, and I don't even get a letter from my wife. So to hell with you. I think I haven't even told you about my new suit, and I won't.

Well give my regards to everybody. Also you might send me a picture of yourself and the children sometime. It's damn ridiculous you can't get some one to make one. My love to you. You might even drop me a line if you get time.

John.

————

MONDAY, JUNE 17

Dear Pen:

Now I'm sorry for all those unkind things I've been saying to you, because on Saturday I got three fine large thick letters from you.

I just learned that I must go to Gdynia again tomorrow to photograph nineteen locomotives arriving by boat. I'll fly. It makes me unhappy, because Thursday is a holiday, Corpus Christi, and we were going to Lowic, a small town 50 miles west, where 100,000 people are expected to be in very huge religious procession. All the peasant women from that part of the country put on their new striped colored skirts that day. I'd planned to shoot some color of it. I've seen these skirts and they really are beautiful. There is a lot of color in Polish country clothing.

Then on Saturday I'm to go to Lublin to photograph the opening of a new hospital.

There are no changes in my situation. I continue to have alternating periods of great despondency, homesickness, longing for wife and children, etc–and doubts and fears as to when they'll send me home. I'm not living a good life in any way–I'm a regular UNRRA man. Irregular meals, considerable vodka–and failing to really get into Poland, either in pictures or in spirit.

I'll have to write to the Shaw Jones and ask them what their stupid sister did with my packet of negatives. That really makes me feel damn bad. It's not so bad to have negatives

John and Brian,
Penny and Ann,
John with Ann and Brian

lying in desk drawers in London as to have them absolutely lost. And with friend Victor skipped – come to think of it, he was awfully casual the way he took my New York address – I had to remind him. I guess I am a damn fool. I'm very sorry I couldn't have had a story about me before I got back. So people would have associated me with Poland. A little touch of something like that would have helped the spirit considerable.

You get me wrong – I am all for UNRRA. It's just me and some of the people who work for it that I view with disrespect. I think UNRRA is really doing a damn fine job of rehabilitation here in Poland.

love
John

———

Monday. July 8

Dear Wife::::

The following things have happened since I wrote you last; I went on a week's trip to Krakow, Kielce, Katowice with Roy Battles of WLW, Cincinnati, and the typical American farmer, the typical American grocer, and the typical American housewife. These four have been touring Europe for a month and are now returning to America to report and broadcast what they have seen and what their impressions are. I will say here and now, I think they probably are typical. And I do not like Americans. America is the greatest of the numerous enemies of progress, peopled with ignorance and arrogance and old bitches gone in the teeth. The typical American housewife, whose name was Mrs. McCarty, from Columbus, Ohio, had a dog, a little teeny black dog which she bought in Germany. And she took it with her, wherever she went. She pressed it to her large breast, and spoke to it. We went through the salt mines outside Krakow. Very interesting. We went through the Wawal Castle in Krakow. The real McCoy, this here castle. And we went to Oswiecem again, and saw the women's hair. And while our guide, a man who'd spent three and a half years there, showed us a brick wall which he said he remembered being all splattered with brains and guts, the typical American housewife cuddled Nixie and said to him, actually addresses this dog of hers – "isn't that awful." Then we went to Czestochowa again, and went in among the worshipping throngs with bugles blowing, drums beating, a very fine show for the devout, and I'll be goddamed if Nixie didn't bark his yapping little throat out at the black madonna Herself.

American radio commentator Roy Battles and Rhea McCarty visiting near Kielce (UNRRA 2461)

Don't try to give me any counter arguments, I know exactly what you would say. So don't say it. This woman is America. And her report to the folks back home, her impression is: I didn't see any evidence of starvation.

I think that if you want to believe fully and earnestly in some thing that makes sense and adds up and is right and good, etc. you haven't much choice. But I do hate every American I know, even more than the average UNRRA English personnel, is the American worse. I think I am now what can be called pro Russian.

Last Sunday, week. Brian and I went around photographing voters. They had a referendum you know. It was very orderly and correctly carried off, which broke Larry Allen's heart, because he had his election riot story all written.

On the 4th of July thirty six of Kielce's hundred and thirty six Jews were stoned to death. About sixty are said to be in the hospital badly beaten up. Anders men were found to have been the leaders in the riot, and were arrested. But still the Americans and the English say: it's a put up job. Trying to blame everything on poor Anders.

Last night Brian and I met a Mr. Hindle, of the *Christian Science Monitor*. He is only the second good correspondent I've met. He isn't really sensible politically, but honest and observant and thoroughly objective. He's nobody's fool, as you would say. And I had a very good conversation with him. Also I might add he looked through my photographs, one by one, every one of them, and was quite impressed, and indicated that when he get back to the US he intended to look into the matter of my pictures in Washington.

A coincidence: I met a guy from Dubuque, so we talked about the only thing I can remember quite well in Dubuque, the Canfield Hotel, the bar there, with the Irish bartender, the restaurant, etc. This guy I met tells me he used to bell hop at the Canfield. So no doubt we are the only two people in all of Poland who have ever even heard of the Canfield in Dubuque. Then. The very next morning. On the front page of the *London Times* I read the story of the Canfield burning to a crisp and fourteen people dying a horrible death. That's a coincidence.

Do you use the car at all? I want to go home and see you and the children and my mother and North Dakota, but then I want to come back. To Paris. I'll get a job from someone while I'm in the States. What about this Stryker Esso thing you once mentioned? I would hastily drop my UNRRA connections if there is something himself would like me to be doing.

Well. this better be a short letter. I'm tired of writing and there isn't much to say anyway.

Love,
John

Ruined shrine in Warsaw (JV 223)

NOTES TO THE LETTERS

1. We lived in Greenbelt, Maryland, from 1939 until 1943. The town was an experiment in co-operative living, run by the U.S. government, just outside Washington, D.C.

2. Polly Wallace was my mother's close friend–possibly her roommate at Oberlin College.

3. Letters from London written in December indicate that he was there, waiting to be sent to Poland, for at least six weeks.

4. I believe that all the letters up to this point were mailed at the same time, starting with the first letter written from Warsaw, actually dated January 10, 1945, which was clearly an error, since the postmark on the envelope reads January 19, 1946, U.S. Army Postal Service A.P.O. There is also a #2 written on the envelope, which suggests that he may not have stuffed all the material into the same envelope, even if they were all mailed on the same day.

5. Roy Stryker was the photography director, or "section chief," of the Farm Security Administration, the government organization in which John began as a file clerk and then gradually was inspired to borrow a camera and begin making his own photographs around Washington. Eventually he joined the photographic staff and was sent on assignment throughout the United States, but with particular emphasis on the Midwest. When Stryker became photography editor for *The Lamp*, which was the promotional magazine published by Standard Oil, John was invited to join the photography staff there, and our family moved to New York City. Penny also worked for Stryker in various clerical and editorial jobs, such as writing captions for photographs.

6. Stefan is crossed out in pencil and written in here, in Penny's handwriting, is "Victor." Also Karmiuski is crossed out. "Holzar or Hattar" and the address are crossed out, and 26 Broadway is written in Penny's handwriting. Also at the bottom of the page a phone number is added in her writing: Hanover 2–3553.

7. Jack and Irene Delano; he was an FSA photographer, she a writer. They were good friends of John and Penny's, a remarkably multitalented couple who later moved to Puerto Rico.

8. Lew Gittler and his wife were family friends. He is frequently referred to throughout these letters. They were Jewish.

9. Esther Bubbly and Sol Libsohn were Standard Oil photographers. Jim Feely was John's best friend from childhood. They grew up together in St. Paul, Minnesota, and moved to Washington, D.C., together. Ann and Brian were his two children, ages seven and four.

10. Phil and Polly Brown had been good friends of my parents in Washington, D.C. I don't believe either one was involved with photography.

11. Les Atkins apparently had worked for Standard Oil, as did his wife, Edie.

12. John's younger brother Robert had worked on a farm in Minnesota for several summers.

13. After basic training, he had spent his army time being taught how to operate a movie camera, in expectation that he would be sent to the front to shoot newsreels. The end of the war changed that.

14. Ed Rosskam was a Farm Security Administration photographer.

15. Marion Post Wolcott was a Farm Security Administration photographer.

16. The Exquisite Corpse, a form of artistic collaboration devised by the Dadaists, in which a sheet of paper is folded in such a way that each person contributes part of the drawing without being able to see the rest, except for certain guiding lines.

17. John Collier was a Farm Security Adminstration photographer who also moved to New York to work for Stryker at Standard Oil. He later moved to the southwest where he became very involved with Native Americans.

18. The photographic department of Standard Oil, directed by Roy Stryker, where Penny worked. Sol Libsohn, Gordon Parks, and Esther Bubbly were all photographers. Sally Forbes also worked in the office. Penny's letters must have made references to her, since they became good friends.

19. Arnold Eagle was another photographer. The Standard Oil offices were at Rockefeller Plaza.

20. This was the system used in the Farm Security files, still evident in the Library of Congress collection. John was reputed to have devised it, when he worked as a file clerk for the FSA, but this may just be family folklore. At the United Nations I found the UNRRA photographs filed in contact-size prints. These were approximately 3″ by 5″, since they had been shot with a Speed Graflex.

21. I remember the jacket and suspect that either the pants never fit right or something. The fabric was a rich tobacco-colored tweed, with flecks of bright orange and blue. Very nice, but a rather loose weave, so that the jacket didn't hold its shape well and always looked pretty baggy.

22. Dorothea Lange was another Farm Security Administration photographer, best known for her pictures of migrant farm workers in California.

23. Her real name was Emily Millicent. Her family always called her Millicent, and Penny became her nickname at college, because Millicent ends with "cent" and a cent is a penny. John always liked to make up strange names when he wrote letters, both for the addressee and for himself.

POLAND IN BLACK AND WHITE

PHOTOGRAPHS, 1946

Snowy Street, Warsaw

Destroyed Train Station, Warsaw

Women Salvaging Bricks, Gdansk

Boy with Crutch

Ruined Skyscraper, Warsaw

95

Busy Corner, Warsaw

St. Alexander Church, Warsaw

97

Reconstruction of the Opera House, Warsaw

Horse in Archway

Woman Eating Soup, Laski

Soup Kitchen, Warsaw

Makeshift Clothing Store, Warsaw

Selling Radishes, Warsaw

Blind Woman

Women Selling Bread, Warsaw

Russian Soldiers

U.S. Troop Train

The Eyes of Poland

Changing Trains

Administering First Aid

Shrine on a Boxcar

Barefoot Girl

Man with Accordion

Repatriate Family in Boxcar with Stove

Repatriate Family in Boxcar Doorway

Repatriate Family Living in Boxcar

Gypsy Ladies

Gypsy Children in Boxcar Doorway

Gypsy Girl

Gypsy Children

Woman with Duck

Farmer

Family from Policzna

Two Girls, near Kielce

Two Boys, Policzna

Woman in Doorway of Ruined Farmhouse, Zabocie

Sunday Grooming, Zarzecze

Boy with Cup, Glowaczow

Boy with Bread, Boduen

Landscape with Derelict Car

Remains of Building, Wroclaw

134

Child Passing Ruins, Szydlow

135

Coal Miners

Market Day

Chimney Sweep

Woman with Photograph

Triplets

Boy Demonstrating German Salute

German Deportees, Wroclaw

School Children, Nysa

Peasants Fleeing Burning Village

145

Mother with Child Suffering from Rickets, Olasksow

Mother and Child, Olasksow

Girls Walking Home from School

NOTES TO THE PHOTOGRAPHS

These photographs come from two sources. Prints marked UNRRA, followed by a four-digit number, are from the United Nations Relief and Rehabilitation Administration files in the UN Archives, New York City. The back of each print is stamped "Received from UNRRA Visual Information Office, Washington, under agreement of March 10, 1947, by U.N. Dept. of Public Information, Visual Information Center. Catalogued by U.N. Archives. Property of the United Nations. Credit: UNRRA Photograph from United Nations." Each photograph bears a caption, and some identify the photographer; others are rubber-stamped "Photo–John Vachon." I have usually included the entire caption in these notes, indicated by quotation marks. Sometimes I have only used excerpts in order to eliminate repetition. Prints marked JV, followed by a three-digit number, are from John Vachon's personal collection of prints and negatives, currently in my possession.

P. 91 Snowy Street, Warsaw, JV 135. This building is now the Museum of Ethnography on corner of Kreditova Street and Mazowiecka.

P. 92 Destroyed Train Station, Warsaw, JV 129. The ruins of the brand new train station that was Warsaw's pride are seen from a window in the Hotel Central.

P. 93 Women Salvaging Bricks, Gdansk, UNRRA 2329. "February 1946. Women of Gdansk removing bricks from destroyed building."

P. 94 Boy with Crutch, JV 309.

P. 95 Ruined Skyscraper, Warsaw, JV 133. Before the war this was Warsaw's only skyscraper, with a radio antenna on top. It was a commercial building, built by the Prudential Insurance Company, and the tallest building in Poland. It is now the Hotel Warszawa, on Pl. Powstancow Warszawy.

P. 96 Busy Corner, Warsaw, JV 134. This photograph was taken from the Hotel Polonia, possibly from the roof, at the corner of Aleja Jerozolimskie and Marszalkowska Streets, where businesses were thriving in new shop fronts built since the war.

P. 97 St. Alexander Church, Warsaw, JV 409. This historic church still stands on the Square of Three Crosses in Warsaw, near the American Embassy at the beginning of Aleje Ujazdowskie. It was rebuilt after the war without the two towers, one of which is seen in this photograph. The towers were not part of the original structure.

P. 98 Reconstruction of the Opera House, Warsaw, JV 343. Women working to repair the Teatr Wielki, or Great Theater. The segment of the building shown in this photograph has been rebuilt and extended beyond these original dimensions.

P. 99 Horse in Archway, JV 132.

P. 100 Woman Eating Soup, Laski, UNRRA 4487. "Mrs. Rakowska shares a cellar with her son and daughter-in-law and three small children in the village of Laski. They, too, have only potatoes to eat."

P. 101 Soup Kitchen, Warsaw, UNRRA 4670. "Soup kitchen in Warsaw, Poland, operated by the government for the very poor. Children come here each day at noon, bringing their own pails or containers, and receive a hot lunch made up in part of UNRRA-supplied food."

P. 102 Makeshift Clothing Store, Warsaw, JV 218. The writing on the building says, "Checked: No Mines." There were many tragedies after the war ended, both in cities and in the countryside, from exploding mines. A note on the negative envelope in Penny Vachon's hand reads, "Posnenska Street, Warsaw—Clothing shop in doorway of destroyed building."

P. 103 Selling Radishes, Warsaw, JV 220.

P. 104 Blind Woman, JV 484.

P. 105 Women Selling Bread, Warsaw, JV 127.

P. 106 Russian Soldiers, JV 266.

P. 107 U.S Troop Train. No negative exists for this print.

P. 109 The Eyes of Poland, UNRRA 2422. Vachon considered this possibly the finest photograph he had ever made and gave it this title. It is a group of repatriates gathered around outside a train car in which people were singing what he believed was a Polish national anthem. The caption in the UN files reads, "Poland, March 1946. Farm hands en route from Siberia to the recovered lands of Western Poland."

P. 110 Changing Trains, JV 187. A similar photograph in the UN files is captioned "Polish Repatriates from Russia–March 1946. Transferring household goods from broad-gauge Russian train on the right to standard gauge Polish train on the left, at Mikulczyce railroad junction, near Katowice." Ana Maria Dembinska is in the lower left corner. A caption on another photograph of the same scene reads, "Taken near the City of Katowice in the district of Slask Dabrowski, Upper Silesia."

P. 111 Administering First Aid, JV 366. Based on information gleaned from other photographs, I believe this is a Red Cross worker applying first aid to one of the repatriates, while the transfer of families is occurring from one train to another.

P. 112 Shrine on a Boxcar, JV 185. The Polish flag and a picture of the Virgin and Child are decorated with branches of a fir tree on the exterior of this boxcar carrying repatriates from the "lost territories" to Silesia.

P. 113 Barefoot Girl, JV. No negative exists for this print.

P. 114 Man with Accordion, UNRRA 4734. "Poland–May, 1946. All their worldly goods are stacked inside and on the roof of a boxcar on a repatriation transport from Rudki, which is carrying them to a farm in Upper Silesia."

P. 115 Repatriate Family in Boxcar with Stove, UNRRA 4735. "Poland, May 1946. A Polish peasant family of repatriates from Rudki, southwest of Lwow, in their boxcar during the 11-day journey to Silesia."

P. 116 Repatriate Family Living in Boxcar, UNRRA 4679. "All their worldly goods are stacked inside and on the roof of a boxcar on a repatriation transport from Rudki, which is carrying them to a farm in Upper Silesia. The journey has already taken 9 days."

P. 117 Repatriate Family in Boxcar Doorway, JV. No negative exists for this print.

P. 118 Gypsy Ladies, JV 486.

P. 119 Gypsy Children in Boxcar Doorway, JV 149.

P. 120 Gypsy Girl, JV 327.

P. 121 Gypsy Children, JV 339.

P. 123 Woman with Duck, JV 400.

P. 124 Farmer, UNRRA 2619. "At 75, Kaminski is working the soil he loves at Szatki, north of Warsaw. Patching has helped keep his tattered garments together, and his gloves aren't mates, but his look of determination will never wear out." Another photograph that includes him is identified as the Kaminski farm, near Pultusk. They have built a shed for the horse, and the family sleeps in a German dugout.

P. 125 Family from Policzna, UNRRA 4468. "Stanislaw Zakrzewski and his wife, Bronislawa, were forced by the Germans to leave their farm in the village of Policzna. They returned in 1945 with their four young children, only to find their livestock and farm tools gone, their house completely destroyed and the land covered with bomb craters and mines, unfit for cultivation even had they any seed. From lack of nutrition, the children's skin and teeth are poor and their legs badly formed."

P. 126 Two Girls, near Kielce, JV 231. These two girls are also seen in UNRRA 2461, which reads, "Peasant children in fly-ridden kitchen of their shack near Kielce. This family had not eaten meat for several months. Bread and potatoes were its principal diet." They are also in the photograph with Roy Battles and the American lady with the dog.

P. 127 Two Boys, Policzna, JV 177. These are brothers from the Zakrzewski family. Note the apparently frozen look of horror on the older boy's face, almost identical to his expression in an earlier photograph. Another photograph of these boys in the UN files states, "A diet of a few potatoes and wild green leaves a day is not conducive to good health."

P. 128 Woman in Doorway of a Ruined Farmhouse, Zabocie, UNRRA 4247. "May, 1946, Tesciowa stands in the door of her old farm building in Zabcie near Pultusk. Her house was shelled when the front line was nearby. Her husband was taken to Germany where he was killed by the Germans." Tesciowa means mother-in-law in Polish.

P. 129 Sunday Grooming, Zarzecze, UNRRA 4461. "Used clothes from the U.S. become this family's Sunday best. Once prosperous, with a fine farm house and a good farm, the Larzycki family salvaged enough planks and bricks from the German destruction to build this one room, grass roofed house."

P. 130 Boy with Cup, Glowaczow, UNRRA 5845. "This young boy of Glowaczow, Poland, looks to UNRRA for help." The photographer is not identified on the print in the UN files. I believe it is Vachon's because of other pictures of this boy that are attributed to him and because I remember seeing a print of it in our house when I was a child.

P. 131 Boy with Bread, Boduen, UNRRA 4362. "Wincenty Rakowski, 8 years old, whose parents were killed by the Germans. UNRRA wheat and other foodstuffs are eaten by the orphans at Boduen. Two loaves are the daily ration for 6 people."

P. 133 Landscape with Derelict Car, UNRRA 4421. "Wrecked war transport is scattered about the fields. A typical scene in Silesia where the Jaroszewicz family and hundreds of thousands of other repatriates are farming the land in preparation for the vital harvest of 1946." This photograph bears a striking resemblance to Vachon's FSA photography of the Midwest, particularly North Dakota.

P. 134 Remains of Building, Wroclaw, JV 240. A German advertisement for soap flakes once adorned this building in the city formerly known as Breslau.

P. 135 Child Passing Ruins, Szydlow, UNRRA 4732. "A little girl wandering through a ruined street in the village of Szydlow, Poland."

P. 136 Coal Miners, JV 158. A related photograph, UNRRA 2371, describes miners waiting for the skip (elevator) to take them 200 meters underground to the General Zawadzki mine. One of the miners is identified as Zenon Polak.

P. 137 Market Day, JV 168.

P. 138 Chimney Sweep, JV 263.

P. 139 Woman with Photograph, JV 164. A woman is sitting beneath a photograph of a soldier in the uniform of the Polish Legion, an organization formed after World War I, when Poland was not allowed to form an army. The scene is typically Polish, with various religious and patriotic symbols on the wall.

P. 140 Triplets, JV 168.

P. 141 Boy Demonstrating German Salute, JV 323.

P. 142 German Deportees, Wroclaw, JV 105. Germans deportees carrying their possessions to the train station in Wroclaw. The banner in the background reads, "Polish Party Workers," the precursor of the Polish communist party, according to Dembinska.

P. 143 School Children, Nysa, UNRRA 4425. "Polish school children in Nysa, Silesia, hoes and rakes over their shoulders, start off for a day's work in the fields–part of the desperate effort being made in Poland to prepare the land for the harvest of 1946, on which the lives of millions of Poles will depend."

P. 145 Peasants Fleeing Burning Village, UNRRA 4489. "Fire in Polish Village of Wawolnica, 2 May, 1946."

P. 146 Mother with Child Suffering from Rickets, Olasksow, UNRRA 4479. "Helena Borowska had a comfortable home with her husband and two young daughters, 11 and 8 years old, in the village of Olasksow. It was a village of 300 houses. But all the inhabitants were driven out by the Germans and on their return in March 1945, they found only ten houses left. Today most of the people are living in cellars of the destroyed buildings. Mr. Borowski is a tailor, but now he has no material to work with and none of the villagers could buy from him if he had. The farms about the village are non-productive for lack of all that is necessary to operate a farm. The people must live as best they can on a few potatoes and wild leaves. One-year-old Stanislaw has rickets, and is very weak from lack of food. The other children of the village have poor teeth and skin. They all suffer from malnutrition."

P. 147 Mother and Child, Olasksow, JV 393.

P. 149 Girls Walking Home from School, JV 316.

AFTERWORD

ANN VACHON

I was eight when my father went to Poland, made these pictures, and wrote the letters to my mother. My strongest memory of his absence is that he was gone for Christmas, which everyone seemed to think was very sad for the children. He came back and told us what wonderful people the Poles were, how fine, and musical, and devout, and somehow extremely dignified. Sometimes we would dance to the one Polish record he had brought back–something with a refrain we sang along with: "Bumpshebula, Bumpshebula, Ayayayay," although we probably got it all wrong. The photographs were never published to the extent he'd hoped–they never made him famous. One picture, of peasants fleeing from a burning village against a sky of billowing smoke, was highly honored; it was printed in *U.S. Camera* and bought and hung by the Museum of Modern Art. Of this my father was extremely proud, though he never thought of himself as an artist, rather a photojournalist.

John (which was what his kids called him) was a faithful letter writer all his life, a habit he had more or less inherited from his traveling salesman

Ann Vachon, summer of 1946

father, Harry, along with a drinking problem. A difference was that Harry acknowledged his problem, and wrote daily to his wife when he was on the road, to let her know that all was well and he was sober. John believed for most of his life that his own drinking was under control, and he wrote letters because he loved to write. In fact his real life's ambition was to be a novelist–and he actually completed a novel about a traveling salesman, but never found an interested publisher. At any rate, his interest in writing found an outlet in letters. After his death we discovered two trunks full of letters, to his mother and to his first wife, (my mother) Penny. He'd naturally expected both of them to save his letters, and there is evidence that he'd sorted through the ones written to my mother some time after her death, and organized them into packets marked by the year they were written.

So he'd wanted to be a writer, or else maybe a famous movie star. (I discovered this from his early, adolescent journals. As he was dying of cancer, in 1974, he suggested that I might want to read his journals after he died. "Why not now, so we can talk about them?" I asked. Well, he wasn't so sure about that, so I waited.) He also had written a dozen short stories, mostly related to his own growing up in the Midwest. When I was in high school, and my friends and I wanted to grow up to be writers, I snuck his stories out of the house to show my best friend. She thought they were wonderful, and that I was really lucky to almost have J. D. Salinger for a father!

John was born and raised in St. Paul, Minnesota, in a mostly Irish household; he was an altar boy and went to Catholic schools right through college. Then he moved to Washington, D.C., to attend Catholic University. Unfortunately he broke their rules, did some illicit drinking, and got thrown out, though it was a while before he wrote this information home to his mother.

So there he was in Washington, D.C., without a job during the Depression. Hoping to find interesting work, he really didn't want a government job. But he couldn't afford to be choosy, so he accepted a position as a lowly file clerk, working for a man named Roy Stryker, who directed the Farm Security Administration photographic documentation project. He had no previous interest in photography himself, but his work exposed him first to the work and then to the photographers–Walker Evans, Ben Shahn, Dorothea Lange, Russell Lee, Marion Post Wolcott, Arthur Rothstein, and others. Eventually Roy encouraged him to borrow a camera for the weekend, and see what he could do. He got some advice from Evans and Shahn in particular, and pretty soon was being sent out on assignments himself.

The FSA photographers, under Stryker's leadership, were creating a powerful documentation of this period in the United States. They traveled all over the country, primarily visiting rural areas, but also covering Chicago stockyards, Michigan meat plants, and soup kitchens from San Francisco to the Bowery. Perhaps the most well-known images from these files were of migrant workers in California, and dust-bowl refugees from Texas and Oklahoma.

In Washington he met my mother, three years his elder, a Phi Beta Kappa graduate of Oberlin College, and a pianist, intellectual, and agnostic. She had been raised in a fairly strict Methodist family just outside of Pittsburgh. They fell in love, got married, informed their disapproving parents, and eight months later I was born–six weeks early, if anyone was counting. My brother Brian was born three years later, and Gail came after the war, in 1948.

John traveled around the United States from 1937 until shortages of gasoline and rubber for tires, due to the war, curtailed the photographic project. He kept a county map of the United States, and every time he came home from one of his trips, he'd fill in every county he'd entered with red ink. He loved crossing borders, as is evident in these letters, and for a long time the only state he'd never entered was Nevada. He kept other kinds of records of his travels, too–a list of every place he'd ever had a haircut, for instance.

He particularly loved the Midwest, and especially the Dakotas and Minnesota, which had been his father's territory as a traveling salesman of stationery. He photographed grain elevators, front porches, snow fences, billboards, mailboxes and telephone wires, farmers wives making preserves, unemployed men napping on park benches, kids trudging through snow with flapping galoshes, nightclub singers in Des Moines, steel workers lined up for paychecks, and people of all ages, sizes, and attitudes. Mostly the people in his pictures look content, even if their clothes are shabby. He didn't seem to specialize in the pitiful.

He briefly continued working for the government, for the Office of War Information, and then followed Stryker to Standard Oil. Our family moved to New York City in 1943, and both my parents began to work for Standard Oil, my mother writing captions and my father as a photographer. He went to Venezuela on his first major assignment out of the country.

Drafted in 1944, he went through basic training, then had some further instruction on newsreel photography, but apparently struck some sort of deal, because he went to work for UNRRA instead of becoming a soldier. So he flew to London in November 1945, and spent almost two months waiting to see Poland.

These photographs from Poland remind me of his FSA work, except that I think they're better. Some of the early FSA work is poorly focused or framed–he was still learning on that job. In these pictures there seems to be a certain optimism. The people don't look miserable, because he didn't see them as miserable. I think he must have made friends with most people whose pictures he took, even if this had to be done without language, so

John resting on a ladder

that by the time he shot his photos, they trusted him. He was a friendly and very likable guy, with a sincere and serious interest in people.

Unfortunately his letters are my only source of information about this period, and they get somewhat scanty on details toward the end. I can't fill in any missing information about the end of his stay in Europe. A couple of the photographs in the UNRRA files attributed to him are dated August 1946, but I assume those are miscaptioned. When he first returned he talked a lot about our whole family moving to Europe–Switzerland, specifically–so perhaps he traveled there on his way back to the United States. I seem to remember a period of unemployment after he returned, when he was doing some freelance work and very tempted by the idea of remaining a freelance photographer.

His next full-time job, which would last almost until his death in 1975, was as a staff photographer for *Look* magazine. This job sent him all over the world; his map of the places he'd been became filled in with more and more red ink. In 1956 he returned to Poland for a "ten years later" story for *Look*, with text by *Look* correspondent Ed Stevens. This was an opportunity to continue his friendship with Ana Maria Dembinska, who still worked as a translator.

By that time I was seventeen and committed to a career in modern dance. My teacher and mentor, the Mexican-American choreographer José Limón, traveled with his company to Europe in the fall of 1957. Coincidentally Ana Maria Dembinska traveled with them as a translator throughout Poland. Most of Europe was not ready for modern dance, but the Polish people responded to the repertory with great enthusiasm. Limón was as passionate about Poland as my father had been. He found the people's spirit something he wanted to celebrate in his choreography. Of the two works he choreographed in response to these experiences, one was *Missa Brevis* to music by the Hungarian composer, Zoltan Kodaly, to be performed in the ruins of a bombed cathedral. It was a major work that became part of his repertory, and that was how I joined his company, with which I was to continue performing until 1975.

Limón also made *Dances; in honor of Poznan, Wroclaw, Katowice and Warszawa* to a series of mazurkas by Frederic Chopin. In 1986 I reconstructed this ballet, for my own Philadelphia-based dance company, Dance Conduit. I realized that this dance should be performed in Poland for those audiences that had inspired its creation in the first place. So I went to Poland for a four-week visit during the summer of 1987, with press materials about my dance company and a performance videotape, hoping to interest someone in booking Dance Conduit for a Polish tour. I was also interested in seeing Poland for myself and meeting these people that had impressed both my father and my dance mentor so deeply.

One week before I left, it occurred to me that it would be interesting to bring some of my father's 1946 photographs with me. I went to the United Nations archives for the first time and spent an afternoon immersed in this utterly different time and place, fascinated, feeling as transported as if I were watching a feature film. I was intrigued to find that my father's well-known fire photograph had been taken in a village called Walwolnica, and that there were many other shots of that same fire. Many of the photos had captions that included names, and since some of the children had been about my own age, I thought it might even be possible to find some of them now.

When I asked if I could order copies of some pictures, I was told that unfortunately this would take several weeks. But for the first of many times, someone was exceptionally helpful, and allowed me to bring the negatives directly to the photo lab for reproduction. I was able to pick up the prints on the day I left.

With the envelope of photographs under my arm, I went to the Polish consulate to get my visa. While there it occurred to me to visit the cultural attaché, a distinguished gentleman who had attended my company's premiere performance of the "mazurkas." He was not there, but I was ushered upstairs, fussed over a bit, offered tea and petit fours, and then sat down with three important-looking men. What could they do for me? I was suddenly flustered and unprepared, since I had no formal business. So I said that I had simply wanted to show these photographs to the friendly attaché, and I opened the packet.

At this point the pictures were passed from hand to hand, at first in silence, but then the men began to speak–quickly, excitedly, nervously–all, of course, in Polish. One of them asked, rather brusquely I thought, if I had my passport, and I explained that it was still downstairs, getting the visa stamped into it. He sent someone to get it. I began to get rather nervous. They couldn't confiscate my passport, I was sure. But could they refuse to give me a visa? But in a few minutes I received the passport, and this same man explained gruffly that it had been marked in such a way to "assure that I would have a very good time in Poland." (Several weeks later I discovered that this actually freed me from spending the fixed daily amount of hard currency, so that I was free to exchange my dollars privately, and live a very wealthy life while in Poland.) I'm not sure if I said anything to these gentlemen about my dance company. They gave me several names and addresses of people to contact in Warsaw who would be interested in these photographs. But that was not the purpose of my trip.

Polish is not an easy language to learn, and I am not very good at learning languages. I had decided not to even try. But on my overnight train ride from Vienna I shared a couchette with a woman who spoke only Polish. We smiled at each other, and she shared her grapes. Then we smiled at each other and she shared her sausage. We got out of each other's way to prepare for bed. We woke up in the middle of the night to show our passports to the brusque border police. In the morning when she offered to share her sweet rolls with me, I felt terribly empty handed. I hadn't even learned *Dien kouya* for "thank you." So I took out the photographs—one tangible thing I could share with her. She sat looking through them, and I saw tears, one after the other, seep out of her eyes and roll down her face. I began to realize that these pictures meant more than I knew.

I arrived in Warsaw, and knew from a guidebook exactly which inexpensive hotel I would try to find. At the desk a clerk who spoke a little English explained that I had arrived in Poland on the first day of an international conference of the leaders of all the Soviet and Socialist governments—and that every hotel room in the city had been booked far in advance. His recommendation was that I try the city park, which had a campground! I had two heavy bags with me, so I hailed a taxi, and showed him the paper on which the name of the campground was written. We drove for a few blocks, and then he pulled over and turned around to talk to me. "You like camping?" he asked, in hesitant English. I explained that the hotels were all full. He knew all about that, but didn't seem to think the campground was such a good idea, and finally he proposed that he bring me home to his mother's apartment. And so I stayed as their guests for almost four weeks, using it as a base when I traveled to other parts of the country. Although they spoke no English or French or even German, and we therefore had no verbal communication at all, she mothered me with soup and sausage, drew me hot baths when I'd been out all day, and insisted on calling her son the taxi driver to take me to the train station whenever I went out of town.

In Warsaw I went to PAGART (the official government concert tour bureau) and talked to all the right people. But there was merely polite interest in a dance company I could only describe. The videotapes I'd brought with me were in a useless format. Yet when I casually mentioned the photographs I also had with me, the office staff suddenly became extremely interested. One young woman in particular didn't seem to want to let them go. She said that these were pictures of a time in Poland's history of which there was no record and which her generation had never seen. She was terribly moved by them, and I promised her that I would send her copies as soon as I got back to the United States. (I did, but I never heard from her again, and have no idea whether or not she ever received them.)

I visited Krakow, Wroclow, Zakopane, Kielce, all place names I recognized from the captions on the photos. And I went to Walwolnica, where the fire had occurred. I wandered around that small town, noticing that there were still a few buildings with thatched roofs— mostly barns, but this still amazed me. I had an instamatic camera with me and took some pictures: a woman feeding her pigs out the back door of her house; the church, up on a hill; several houses, some with fancy iron grillwork, others with the date they were built worked in stones under the roof peak. I tried some conversation, but it wasn't very productive. I visited a small, local portrait photographer and showed him the pictures of the fire. I think he realized that they were from this town, but there was so little possibility of communication between us that I couldn't be sure. And he would be too young to remember.

I had mentioned to an English-speaking neighbor of my hosts that I would very much like to find the woman, Mary Ann, or Ana Maria Dembinska, who had been my father's good friend and translator in Poland, and who I thought lived somewhere in Warsaw. Telephone books were almost impossible to find, and I was told that the last one had been printed about fifteen years ago. The neighbor thought she recognized the family name and that she might be able to help me. Unfortunately she had assumed a different spelling than the correct one, so it took over three weeks to finally find the telephone number.

When I called, as always nervous about trying to speak on the telephone to someone whose first language was not English, I was greeted effusively, "Oh, John's daughter! Where are you? I will come and see you." So on my very last day in Poland I had lunch with Ana Maria Dembinska. We met at the rather elegant Hotel Victoria, her idea. Then, because I had a great deal of zlotys to spend before leaving, we had a large sumptuous lunch in the hotel restaurant. Ana Maria was in her seventies, yet dressed sportily in shorts and a sleeveless blouse. What I remember most vividly about that first meeting was her astonishing energy. She talked fast and with a greater amount of gesticulation than even I use. It wasn't only her hands that gestured; her arms flailed about, startling waiters and neighboring diners, and her memories and stories came gushing forth, constantly interrupting each other, and often ending with "Oh, maybe that wasn't John. Perhaps that was . . . ," and she would name some other photographer or journalist with whom she had worked. When it was time to catch my train, the taxi driver took us to the station. I gave Ana Maria the last of my zlotys and promised to write.

Several months after I returned to the United States I was mugged, pushed hard from behind, fell splat on my face, and my bag, containing student papers, wallet, and most devastatingly, my address book, was stolen. So I lost all contact with any of the people I'd met in Poland.

Back to work, teaching in the dance department at Temple University and choreographing for my company, I pretty much forgot about those photographs. Until one day I received a phone call at school from a man named Jan Ralph, chief of photography and exhibits at the United Nations. He said that he'd seen my name on the UN archive register and was interested in the research I was doing on my father's work for UNRRA. We planned to meet for lunch. The night before I spent at my stepmother's apartment in Manhattan.

(Françoise Vachon, née Forrestier, had married my father after my mother's death by suicide in 1960, and was now herself working at the United Nations, teaching French. She
and John had two children, Christine and Michael.) We took the box of my father's letters
down from their closet shelf, and from the packet from 1946 I randomly pulled one out. It
described in vivid prose his experiences on a train with repatriates. Françoise encouraged
me to take the letters home with me.

Jan is a photography enthusiast, and was very excited about these pictures. He had a
remarkable story to tell of personally discovering a long-lost cache of UNRRA photographs
taken in China by another former FSA photographer, Arthur Rothstein, at this same time—
photos of which Rothstein had long lamented the loss, and which he was able to publish
in a handsome edition that appeared shortly before his death. Now Jan was eager to do
something with this newly discovered material, particularly after reading the letter I
showed him. He wanted me to prepare a presentation for an organization of photography
professionals called the "Circle of Confusion."

So I brought the letters home and began to transcribe them. I spent Christmas with my
family in New York, and when I was getting ready to leave Françoise suggested that I take
the rest of John's letters, too—the carefully ordered trunk of letters to Penny, and the chaotic
jumble of letters to his mother. We also discovered a box of about two hundred negatives
from Poland and another one full of assorted prints. I brought all these boxes home, feeling
some concern about the responsibility, and wondering who would be interested in really
doing something with them.

But Jan Ralph was persistent. I gave him the additional negatives I'd discovered, and he
had contact prints made, as well as some enlargements. Because the pictures had all been
shot with a Speed Graflex and a Rolleiflex, the contact prints were immediately interesting.
With the help of Harry Amdor, at Modernage Photo Laboratories, we put together a slide
presentation with narration, out of which this book has grown.

Transcribing these letters was often disorienting. Sometimes I became the letter writer,
identifying with the writer, my father, and other times I was my mother, the recipient. But
of course I was always myself, almost twenty-five years older than either of them. And
possibly in some ways a little wiser. It was difficult not to become occasionally disgusted
with John for his insensitivity to his wife. Although on first reading I had been charmed
by the letters, closer scrutiny revealed some rather unpleasant character traits. Also, his
excessive use of alcohol seemed terribly obvious—though I'm not sure it would to an unin-
formed reader. How much should I leave intact, and where should I soften the edges, to
make John come across as the basically fine person I knew him to be? Obviously there

was some personal stuff that would have little interest except for the most prurient of readers, and other boringly repetitive or mechanical material.

The letters certainly threw some new light on my parents' relationship, but they raised more questions than they answered. Unlike my friends' parents, mine had been a physically demonstrative couple, and I don't remember major arguments. I do remember times when my mother in tears on the telephone begged John to come home, when he was out somewhere, drinking. She was never a very happy person, subject to deep depression and anxiety that finally led to psychiatric care, hospitalization, and eventually suicide. But the severity of these problems emerged several years later, after a hysterectomy followed by electroshock therapy. I never thought her marriage was the source of her pain.

So I made some choices. I left in some of his strange misspellings and all of his unusual syntax. There are few actual deletions. Sometimes, but not always, I eliminated names of people he lambasted. If in every single letter he asked for money and stamps, I cut that in half. Sometimes I left out long complex references to their life together, except when it related to his photographic career or seemed to be a telling symptom of the homesickness that he was experiencing.

I began to amass a lot of information about these photographs. The captions on the UNRRA prints provided the most material, but there were also deductions I was able to make from what I read in the letters. I went back to the UN files to do more research, and discovered I could glean information from captions even if I wasn't interested in the particular picture.

I have been living with the photographs for almost seven years now. They have acquired a certain familiarity. Some were already part of my personal "mythology" because I'd known them since childhood. One farmer, dressed in rags, had been looking at me with kind, intelligent eyes all my life, first on the wall in our family dining room, and now more recently in a print I'd given my husband. I've really come to know him and was excited to discover that he was a figure in other pictures. I saw him rebuilding his farm, starting with a barn, while his family lived in temporary shelter in nearby ruins. There was the layout of the compound, there was the pile of fresh lumber, and there was his son. I learned his name and age and the area he lived in from captions on the pictures, but it was the expression on his face that remains with me.

Gradually I began to gather definite identifications for a majority of the photographs. But I was tantalized by a group that I'd found among personal photos. These were clearly the UNRRA personnel, partying, marrying, picnicking. I could only recognize my father and Brian Moore in these pictures. Much as I tried to compare what I'd read in the letters with these photos, I was only guessing at the identities. I felt a definite need to discover who each of these people was, even though the photographs were only snapshots and probably didn't belong in this book.

I had despaired of ever finding Ana Maria Dembinska again—it had taken me four weeks the first time I was in Poland. Now she must be in her eighties, and might be impossible to find. Realistically I knew that she might even have died or become too debilitated with age to help me, but it was difficult to imagine the vital woman I had met in 1987 any less energetic. I began to feel that a trip to Poland would be worthwhile if I could track her down.

The Polish Embassy was helpful; Warsaw had a new telephone book! They gave me a phone number and address for an A. Dembinska, so I wrote at once. Then I became impatient and called. The phone was answered by a young girl—in Polish of course. I said "Ana Maria Dembinska please" very slowly and clearly, and she answered with a lot of Polish. I hung up. Now I was worried—I knew that she had no children herself, but also that she shared her apartment with someone else. Was it a family? Or had she died, and now these other people had moved in? Or was this the wrong person altogether? It took me a week to find someone to make another phone call for me, someone who could speak Polish. This time we learned that Ana Maria had not lived there for five years. They had no more information. This was not encouraging news, but I couldn't give up—I'd already started to look into airfare to Poland! I called the embassy again, and gave a different spelling of her name. No use. I called again. And then somehow suddenly they found an Ana Maria Dembinska in the phone book, complete with phone number and address. I called immediately, and there she was, full of her special vigor, saying "Oh yes, John's daughter. Where are you?"

So I went back to Poland. I didn't realize until after I'd booked my flight that I was arriving on John's birthday—and Chopin's. I wanted to stay in the Hotel Polonia, for obvious reasons, but couldn't get through to make a reservation. This time I was not going to arrive without a booked room! I brought copies of almost all of the photographs with me, as well as my transcript of John's letters. My plan was to spend most of my time with Ana Maria, possibly traveling outside Warsaw to identify some of the photos I hadn't yet been able to recognize.

Ana Maria was fantastic and eager about our project. I started by showing her the photos of the UNRRA personnel, and she was immediately able to identify several of them. She was always ready to hazard a guess, however, even if the next day she revised it. I decided we should only work with the photographs for a few hours each day—I knew from experience how blurry-eyed one can get from spending too much time with them. I also gave her the manuscript to read, thinking it would help to recall that time period. The second day she confessed that she'd stayed up till dawn the night before, reading it.

My favorite pastime in Warsaw, sometimes undertaken alone and sometimes with Ana Maria, was wandering the streets looking for familiar landmarks from the photos. I saw so many buildings that looked as if they were built before 1946, because Warsaw rebuilt after the war as closely as possible to the original. I had remembered that this was true in the historic old city, but now found it so all over Warsaw. The only difference is that what may originally have been stone buildings were now fashioned out of concrete. So I would carry a packet of photographs with me, and stop to count windows, or examine whether the pillars were Ionic or Corinthian. It was a very satisfying detective game, although most of my discoveries would have been quite obvious to anyone who really knew the city. For example, I thrilled to discover that the Hotel Warszawa was precisely as many stories tall and windows wide as a photograph John had made of a bombed ruin. Later I discovered that this building was a well-known landmark–it had been the highest building in Poland before the war, and some said the highest in all Europe. It had been built by the Prudential Insurance Company. Churches were easier to identify. I sometimes had some information from a caption on the photograph, such as a street name. At one point I was certain that my print had been made backwards because of a certain curve of the street, until I discovered a particular third story iron balcony that enabled me to find the exact site from which that picture had been shot.

We visited the Warsaw Museum, four floors in which hundreds of years of history are documented and illustrated. Our visit began with a viewing of a potent film with footage of the destruction of Warsaw. Until then I hadn't actually realized how purposeful and brutal it had been, a systematic retaliation for the Varsovian uprising after years of German occupation. I was deeply affected by the film and wondered at the power of visual media. I returned the next day and was able to meet with Anna Topolska, a photography curator at the museum. She had a wonderful eye, and she could look at a picture and either identify it immediately or close her eyes and recall a location, check with her mental image, and then make a conjecture. She was also thrilled by my collection, particularly the photographs of Warsaw, and I promised her I would send a complete set when I had a chance to have more prints made. But she was little help with photos from other cities in Poland, since she has not traveled herself that much. Also I realized that many of the other cities, particularly Poznan and Gdansk, had not rebuilt the old structures, but demolished the ruins and created new modern buildings as replacements.

Ana Maria had some interesting things to say about John. I remember one of the first things she had said when I'd originally met her was that she and John had never had an affair. Now she spoke of his being "in love" with Stella (of the letters), but also of his homesickness. In some ways I realized that it wasn't such a good idea to have shown her the letters right away, because it colored her memory. But mostly it was useful. For example, in one of our early conversations she told me the story about the time they were picnicking in the countryside and arrested. She said that their jeep was both followed and led by army vehicles, but that their driver knew there were snipers in the woods and was afraid they'd be shot at if they were seen driving with the militia, so he'd pulled ahead of the forward car and sped to Krakow, arriving well in advance of their armed guard. I couldn't quite figure out why John had written about that incident so differently–the soldiers all piling into their car, not letting them speak English, his sketch of the bullet belt. Then the next day, after reading his version, she realized she was remembering another occasion, probably with someone else.

Often her stories would start with John, but as they developed I realized that she was talking about one of the many photographers and journalists she had befriended over the years. She had remained close to the Shaw Jones family and knows both children and their families now. John had invited her to his wedding when he married Françoise in Paris in 1960, but she was unable to get out of Poland at that time. She did meet John and Françoise and their children as well as my daughter Laura, who was traveling with them in about 1969. She told me about a regular newsletter that Dick Baradel had been sending her for many years every Christmas, in which he reported on the lives of all the UNRRA personnel with whom he'd been able to remain in contact. Often I had trouble following her stories since they were so peopled with historical figures I didn't recognize and assumed were personal friends, and sometimes because I wouldn't realize that a tangent was about someone's brother or son rather than the person himself. Still they were always fascinating, even when I was lost.

About John she said, "He was such a good person–and so terribly sad." That really surprised me the first time she said it. What did she mean? I had always thought of him as easy going and full of life. I'm still not certain whether it was a profound insight, or something that she arrived at after reading these letters, or the impression she was left with after her last encounter with him, in Paris, when he'd gotten terribly drunk, and no one could find him for several days. Although this was a rare occurrence, it had happened two or three times during his last years of life. When he was diagnosed as having cancer, he received chemotherapy, and at one point a blood transfusion, from which he contracted hepatitis. This forced a sobriety upon him that allowed a death of greater dignity than we had come to expect.

She was upset about some of the things John had written in his letters. He'd called her his "best Polish anti-Semitic friend," and she protested that label vehemently, really quite hurt by it. He had also referred to her as "extremely non-beautiful," but we both agreed that he must have said that to protect my mother from feeling jealous. She told me that at first she and Brian Moore couldn't stand each other–Brian had a very brusque manner and she found him offensive–but John kept insisting they would appreciate each other. They resisted for some time, but finally ended up quite good friends after all.

Of course in my wanderings I went to find the Hotel Polonia and what had been the Hotel Central, which I recognized from the iron balcony showing in the foreground of one of John's shots of the devastated train station. The building still stands, and seems to be offices now, with a billiard parlor on the ground floor.

I spent my last night at the Polonia, intending to get a large room with private bath, which I could imagine duplicated John's precious darkroom. But I decided to save money and take a bathless single instead. Ana Maria and I had drinks that night at the hotel bar, and then ate in the dining room. It was indeed an elegant room, with a ceiling about thirty feet high, but it was gloomy and rather stark, with almost no other diners present. I could see the balcony where musicians would have played, and could imagine couples waltzing. The food was indeed delicious, and I remembered all the sumptuous meals John had described in his letters.

I realized that my detective work had finally come to an end, and yet I knew that this would not be my last visit to Poland. Like my father, I find myself drawn to these people, and I have accepted an invitation to return, this time to teach a choreography workshop at the Ballet Academy. Someday perhaps I may even have a chance to meet some of the people I have come to know so well through these photographs.

171